PICTORIAL HISTORY

PITTWATER

JOAN LAWRENCE

FRONT COVER: Looking over Newport c1960 as photographed by Frank Hurley.
(National Library of Australia)

BACK COVER: Horses pick up goods from a steamer stopping at Newport Wharf in 1904. Note the seaweed drying on the bank.
(Isobel Bennett, Pittwater Library Local Studies)

Kingsclear Books
ABN 99 001 904 034
PO Box 335 Alexandria 1435
kingsclear@wr.com.au
www.kingsclearbooks.com.au

Phone (02) 9557 4367 Facsimile (02) 9557 2337

Design and layout Mel Broe
Index Dianne Harriman

First printed 2006, reprinted with updates 2012
Printed by Everbest, China

APPROXIMATE METRIC CONVERSIONS

1 foot	=	30.48 centimetres
1 yard	=	0.914 metres
1 mile	=	1.609 kilometres
1 gallon	=	4.546 litres
1 ton	=	1016.047 kilograms
1 acre	=	0.404 hectares

ACKNOWLEDGEMENTS

THE author would like to thank Tina Graham from Warringah Library Local Studies and Virginia Macleod from Pittwater Library Local Studies for their assistance with photographs and information. Thanks also to Pittwater and Warringah Councils for permission to use their extensive photographic collections. Thanks to the Mitchell Library, the State Library of New South Wales, State Records, the National Library of Australia, Dixon Library, News Limited, Manly, Warringah and Pittwater Historical Society, NSW Government Printing Office, the Roads and Traffic Authority, Laurie Seaman, Peter Verrills and Carl and Caressa Gonsalves for the use of photographs.

Thanks also to Jim Boyce and Virginia Macleod for reading the manuscript. Lastly I wish to thank Catherine Warne the publisher for the opportunity to write a pictorial history on the unique area of Pittwater.

Commodore Heights

Three Heads

West Head

Barrenjoey Head

Resolute Beach

Great Mackerel Beach

Lambert Peninsula

Palm Beach

Snapperman Beach

Currawong (Little Mackerel Beach)

Cabbage Tree Boat Harbour

COASTERS RESTREAT

Observation Point

Sand Point

PALM BEACH

The Basin

Soldiers Point

KU-RING-GAI CHASE NATIONAL PARK

Dark Gully

Portuguese Beach

Stokes Point

Whale Beach

Pugnose

Careel Bay

Longnose

Paradise Beach

Towlers Bay

Clareville Beach

Woody Point

Lovett Bay

Long Beach

Rocky Point

Taylors Point

AVALON

Scotland Island

Elvina Bay

McCarrs Creek

Bilgola Plateau

BILGOLA HEAD

Salt Pan Cove

Church Point

BIILGOLA

Horse Shoe Cove

Browns Bay

Bayview

Green Point

NEWPORT

Winnejeramy

LEFT: The bays and inlets of Pittwater. (James Young)

OPPOSITE: The local government area of Pittwater. (James Young)

CONTENTS

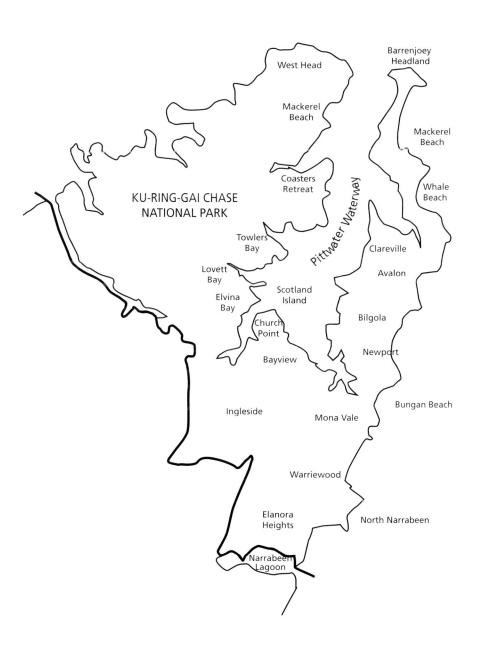

On the map:

Barrenjoey Headland

West Head

Mackerel Beach

Mackerel Beach

KU-RING-GAI CHASE NATIONAL PARK

Coasters Retreat

Whale Beach

Pittwater Waterway

Towlers Bay

Clareville

Lovett Bay

Avalon

Elvina Bay

Scotland Island

Church Point

Bilgola

Bayview

Newport

Ingleside

Mona Vale

Bungan Beach

Warriewood

Elanora Heights

North Narrabeen

Narrabeen Lagoon

LANDFORM

HAWKESBURY sandstone covers most of the Sydney Basin but there is evidence of softer Hawkesbury sandstone in some areas such as on Bushrangers Hill, Newport. The Pittwater headlands are formed of the harder, yellow Narrabeen sandstone. Native eucalypts are believed to have appeared between 24 and 37 million years ago. Once there was rainforest vegetation on the fertile soil on Narrabeen sandstone deposits, now only found in shady, secluded gullies.

Like Port Jackson, Broken Bay and Pittwater are drowned river valleys created when sea levels rose during the last ice age. Once Barrenjoey Headland was attached to West Head by a rock saddle but geological changes opened Pittwater directly to the ocean and the entrance widened and became tidal. Pittwater is some ten kilometres long and its width varies from several hundred metres to nearly three kilometres between Clareville and Towlers Bay.

From the vantage point of West Head Barrenjoey Headland is observed as a tied island, that is a rocky sandstone headland joined to the mainland by a sandspit. At Palm Beach there are high sand dunes at the northern end of the sandspit and an igneous intrusion on the south western side of the headland. The tombolo or sandspit has a beach on each side, namely Palm Beach, and within Pittwater, Barrenjoey Beach. South of Barrenjoey's Shark Rock are Pittwater's largest sea grass beds of *Posidonia australis*. The sea grass is an important habitat for fish and crustaceans.

There is evidence of human occupation of the Sydney Basin 40,000 years ago or even earlier. These early inhabitants probably resided along the coast.

An aerial view showing the landform of Barrenjoey Headland with Pittwater to the right.
(Frank Hurley, National Library of Australia)

ABORIGINAL PITTWATER

THE Aborigines of Pittwater were coastal people who hunted, fished and gathered shellfish and edible plants. Barrenjoey has a long association with Aboriginal settlement. Rocky overhangs provided shelter on the northern side of the headland and many middens (residue of shellfish, animal bones and charcoal from fires) sat in the sand dunes. These later disappeared during periods of bulldozing. In Ku-ring-gai Chase National Park there are hundreds of Aboriginal sites including rock engravings, cave art, grinding grooves and middens.

During the early period of settlement the officers of the First Fleet recorded contact with the Aborigines of the Sydney region, noting their lifestyle, fishing methods and weapons. Some recorded the languages and drew sketches of their encounters. Initially the local people took an interest in the activities of the settlers but as Lieutenant Tench recorded in early February 1788 'The Indians for a little while after our arrival paid us frequent visits, but in a few days they were observed to be more shy of our company'. As some officers had served in the American colonies, they frequently referred to the Sydney residents as 'Indians'.

The name 'Ku-ring-gai' is not mentioned in First Fleet records and is not officially used on the peninsula until 1894. In 1961 F D McCarthy, Curator of Anthropology at the Australian Museum, stated no name had ever been recorded for the people of the peninsula. Peter Turbet in *The Aborigines of the Sydney District before 1788*, published in 1989, makes no mention of Ku-ring-gai but lists the Garigal who 'lived in the Broken Bay–Pittwater area'.

N B Tindale, pioneer of Australian archaeology, favoured the theory that the people of the Pittwater area belonged to the Darug (various spellings). Local historians Shelagh and George Champion in their paper 'Did the Aborigines of the Manly Warringah & Pittwater Peninsula Really Belong to the Ku-ring-gai

Tribe?' state that John Fraser, Fellow of the Royal Society of NSW, was aware of a clan called 'Gringai' near Dungog and changed Gringai to Ku-ring-gai after ten years of thought and inquiry. He claimed their territory stretched from Port Macquarie to Bulli and to the Blue Mountains. He stated Ku-ring-gai meant 'I am Kuri or I am man'. Tindale believed Fraser used the name in an arbitrary fashion and that Fraser coined the name. Val Attenbrow in *Sydney's Aboriginal Past*, published in 2002, only mentions the Garigal. Warren Whitfield, of Aboriginal descent, declared in 2002 at an Aboriginal welcome at the Woy Woy Australia Day celebrations 'They weren't Dharug. They were Wannungine-speaking people, the Guringai of the Walkeloa clan.'

Bungaree, 'Drawn from Life 1831, and on Stone 1834, by Chas. Rodius. Painted by I G Austin, 15 Phillip St, Sydney.' Bungaree died in 1830. (State Library of NSW)

Bungaree
Chief of the Broken Bay Tribe

Dressed in tattered trousers, a discarded military jacket with brass buttons and gold braid and a black, red feathered cocked hat, but with bare feet, Bungaree was a familiar figure in early Sydney. Various colonial artists sketched or painted his portrait. There are 30 versions of the spelling of his name in early records. *In King Bungaree – A Sydney Aborigine meets the great South Pacific Explorers, 1799–1830*, Keith Vincent Smith describes Bungaree as 'flamboyant, intelligent and shrewd. He was an explorer, a go-between, a joker, a beggar, a mimic and a drunkard'. He charmed the settlers with his humour and was something of a diplomat dealing with matters between his own people and the colony's officials.

Before his people's world was shattered by the arrival of the First Fleet, Bungaree's country was Broken Bay and his lifestyle that of a traditional member of his clan. Bungaree, aged 24 years, came to prominence through his association with the 25-year-old Matthew Flinders. He accompanied Flinders on the sloop *Norfolk* to explore the 'Glass-house and Hervey's Bays'. Flinders described him as 'Bungaree, a native, whose good disposition and manly conduct had attracted my esteem'. The voyage lasted six weeks and Bungaree acted as 'interpreter' in contacts with the coastal Aborigines.

The remaining people of Bungaree's Broken Bay group settled in Sydney town around 1800. In 1802 Bungaree joined Flinders on the *Investigator* for his circumnavigation of the continent and again Bungaree was the go-between with indigenous people. Governor King sent Bungaree to the Hunter River settlement as a messenger on several occasions and regarded him as 'the most intelligent' of his race.

Governor Macquarie initiated the practice of awarding certain Aborigines a crescent shaped gorget or breastplate, part of the British military uniform. Macquarie presented one to the Broken Bay man bearing the words 'BOONGAREE Chief of the Broken Bay Tribe 1815'. In 1822 Macquarie described Bungaree as chief of the 'Pitt Water Tribe'.

Macquarie endeavoured to act as a conciliator with the local inhabitants and at Georges Head, now in Mosman, established a farm for Bungaree and his people. In 1815 Macquarie had huts built for them and believed 'they and their families appear to be perfectly Contented'. Bungaree became ill and spent time at the General 'Rum' Hospital, but in November 1815 was present for the visit to Georges Head of the Governor and Mrs Macquarie. The farm was in disrepair by 1821 and in 1825 was dispersed as land grants.

In 1817 Bungaree volunteered for a voyage on the *Mermaid* with Phillip Parker King, who described Bungaree as being 'about forty-five years of age, of a sharp, intelligent and unassuming disposition… '.

Sadly Bungaree succumbed to the settlers' alcohol. The North Shore pioneer Alexander Berry treated Bungaree when he was savagely beaten in a drunken brawl. He later wrote Bungaree was the 'first Native in whom I took an interest' and found him 'a man decidedly of considerable natural talent – very faithful & trust worthy… '.

Keith Vincent Smith states Bungaree was the first Aborigine seen by Europeans to throw a boomerang in the area around Sydney and may have introduced the weapon to Port Jackson. In 1829 Bungaree was observed 'in a state of perfect nudity, except for his red feathered hat' in the Government Domain. His health deteriorated and Bungaree again was admitted to the General Hospital and was then cared for by Father Therry. He died among his people at Garden Island on 24 November 1830 and was buried at Rose Bay beside one of his many wives, Matora. His widow, Cora Gooseberry or Queen Gooseberry, outlived him by some 20 years. She died in 1852 and was buried in the Devonshire Street Cemetery.

EXPLORATIONS NORTH

ON Sunday 2 March 1788 Governor Phillip and his party left Port Jackson to examine Broken Bay by cutter and longboat. Phillip planned a survey of the harbour. On arrival the expedition was met by one man and five women in three 'canoes'. Phillip noted 'the finest piece of water I ever saw', which he named Pitt Water for the British Prime Minister, William Pitt the Younger. During eight days of exploration the party landed on and named Mullet (later Dangar) Island. They endured heavy rain and spent nights under the boats or in tents. The governor observed the local people, noted customs and concluded fish formed the main part of their diet. He found the country 'very high and mostly barren and rocky'. Inclement weather forced Phillip to return.

Mona Vale and Pittwater Roads had their beginnings in Aboriginal pathways. Phillip, Lieutenants Johnston, Bradley and Creswell, six soldiers and Surgeon John White made use of a path to examine the coast northwards after they landed at Manly Cove on 22 August. The next day they reached the south branch of Broken Bay. They met Aborigines and White noted bark shelters, nets, fishing lines, spears, and a superior stone hatchet, water carrying implements and a piece of coarse linen which must have come from 'our people'. The party returned along the coastline and reached Manly Cove on 25 August.

From 6 to 16 June 1789 Phillip, with Captain Hunter and others, again explored to the north seeking arable land. This time 'gal-gal-la' (smallpox) had struck. The Aborigines, already infected by venereal disease, succumbed to this new infection and by May 1789 the settlers discovered bodies of Aborigines in the coves and inlets of Sydney Harbour. It is now believed that over 50 per cent of the population of south eastern Australia perished within three years of European arrival, due to European diseases, long before the white arrivals reached more remote areas.

Having been met by the boats, the party explored the arms of Broken Bay. They camped on Mullet Island where Nagle commented 'I am amazing fond of those mullet,' causing Governor Phillip to joke that Nagle had eaten 18 pounds of fish. They sighted the mighty river the Aborigines called Deerubin and rowed some 20 miles before returning owing to insufficient provisions. Phillip's next excursion from 29 June to 14 July 1789 was to determine the source of the river. Armed with 'musquets' and with knapsacks, the party went by land taking five hours to reach Pittwater while the boats proceeded to Broken Bay. They continued up the river where it divided into two branches, later named the Macdonald and Colo Rivers. The boats continued until some 34 miles above Mullet Island. They noted the immense perpendicular mountains of barren rock and the distress of Aborigines, apparently from lack of food. By 6 July they reached Richmond Hill and estimated the Blue Mountains to be some five or six miles distant. Phillip named the river after Lord Hawkesbury and commented on the fertility of the banks. They landed and fished at Mullet Island and finally with a fair wind returned to Pittwater. These expeditions led to settlement of the Hawkesbury in 1794 and 1795.

A four day land excursion was undertaken in September 1790 by Lieutenants Dawes, Tench and Reverend Johnson to Broken Bay. Tench recorded 'which place we found had not been exaggerated in description, whether its capacious harbour, or its desolate incultivable shores, be considered'.

A frightened Aboriginal woman, recovering from smallpox, encounters Governor Phillip's exploratory party in June, 1789, as depicted by Captain John Hunter. (Mitchell Library, State Library of NSW)

SHELLS, SHINGLES AND TIMBER

THERE was a desperate need for lime to make mortar for buildings, and shells were gathered around Port Jackson and to the north and south of the settlement. Aboriginal shell middens which were sometimes as high as 10 metres were plundered. The shells were brought to today's Millers Point and offloaded at Lime Burner's Wharf where they were burned. In the 1850s and 1860s shells were still being brought from Broken Bay and Pittwater. Traces of shells can be seen in the mortar of historic buildings around Sydney.

The casuarinas, or she-oaks, were felled to make roof shingles. This species was prolific around Broken Bay, Pittwater and the Hawkesbury and shingle cutters set up camps to split the tree trunks. The quiet bush atmosphere was a hive of activity as vast amounts of shingles were cut and shipped to Sydney. Good money was made in the first half of the nineteenth century and the shingle cutters continued their lonely occupation.

Another casuarina was used in colonial furniture and the red or forest-oak species was felled to fuel bakers' ovens as it burned quickly. Many small sailing vessels were being loaded with timber for shipment to Sydney. Often the timber was transported by bullock dray via the old Lane Cove Road and timber was also shipped down the Lane Cove River from Fiddens Wharf (Killara). Hefty bullock drivers quenched their thirst at Blues Point while their load crossed the harbour to Sydney.

The rich haul of fish attracted fishermen. First Fleeters Edward Flinn/Flynn, John Howard and William Nott were all emancipated convicts. Flynn was fishing at Pittwater in 1828, aged 74. Howard, indicted as Thomas Howard, aged 64 in the 1828 census, was a fisherman at 'Pitt street or water'. There was a fish drying business at Snapperman Beach, on the Pittwater side of Palm Beach, operated by Ah Chuney. Heaps of snapper and bream were dried, cured, and shipped in barrels,

reaching as many as 200 barrels in one season.

Martin Burke, 1798 Irish patriot and convict, was a pioneer of Pittwater. One of a number of Irishmen who applied for land on the peninsula, Burke received 50 acres in 1814. Records of land promised or granted reveal well-known names such as Blue Mountains explorer William Lawson, who held 640 acres at today's West Head. The first official Catholic priest, Father Therry, held two grants of 280 and 1200 acres. Macquarie's friend and emancipist Andrew Thompson held the first grant in 1810 of 120 acres on Scotland Island. Robert Campbell junior held the largest block and later sold his 700 acres to D'Arcy Wentworth. Robert McIntosh, a constable, held 200 acres promised by Governor Macquarie in 1817. The Olivers later established themselves at Church Point and on the western shores of Pittwater. Their activities included farming, and establishing vegetable gardens and orchards. They kept poultry and bee hives and were self sufficient. In 1829 Surveyor William Govett found Pittwater 'a beautiful and romantic lake'. Life was simple but hard in the 1800s with the bush environment, the tiny settlements and coastal ships and small vessels transporting people and produce around Pittwater and Broken Bay. The remoteness of Pittwater afforded opportunities for smuggling, illicit stills and other nefarious activities. Smuggled goods (mainly rum) were unloaded far from the control of the law. There were ample hiding places until the goods were transported to Sydney or stowed aboard a departing ship. Some residents, like woodcutter James Toomey, were honest. He rode to Sydney to report his discovery of 100 casks of brandy and other liquor. The goods were seized by the water police and found to be valued at £3,000. The smuggling activities of the 1830s and 1840s led to the establishment of a Customs House at Barrenjoey.

Heavily timbered Pittwater Road as seen by watercolour painter William Andrews c1880. (Dixson Library, State Library of NSW)

TRAVELLING TO PITTWATER

BY 1843 Pittwater was officially designated a port. Newport was a new port and life grew up around it. Land transport was more difficult. In 1832 one option was to travel from Balgowlah via the Jenkins Road, named for a local resident. It continued to Jenkins' 'snug house' near Narrabeen Lagoon, then for several miles past settlers' small farms and dwellings. Careel Bay was 15 miles from Balgowlah, with two small farms and cottages, and Barrenjoey was a distance of 19 miles. Local fishermen would ferry travellers across to Brisbane Water. Some redoubtable travellers occasionally walked from Brisbane Water to Sydney. Alternatively a coastal trader could be hired for the trip northwards. Peter Ellery commenced his punt service at The Spit in the late 1840s giving easier access northwards and to Manly. In 1854 the first excursion ferry service began operations between Sydney and Manly.

Horse-drawn coaches operated from Manly and travellers could stay overnight at the Rock Lily Hotel which was built in 1866 at Mona Vale. The scenery was ever changing with glimpses of Manly and Curl Curl lagoons, distant bush clad hills, brushwood, tall timber, ferny gullies, tiny farms and the excitement of the crossing at Narrabeen Lagoon. Before a bridge was built in the 1880s a ford crossed the lagoon and passengers lifted their feet when water was likely to invade the coach. In 1864 there were calls for the road to Pittwater to be made passable at all times. Barrenjoey and Pittwater Roads were surveyed in 1877. In 1889 the Sydney Tourist Bureau reported the number of

ABOVE: Shingle splitters in Ku-ring-gai Chase National Park c1890s. (Pittwater Library Local Studies)

BELOW: Machon's Sawmill at Natuna Street North Narrabeen, 1930. (Pittwater Library Local Studies)

passengers sent by that office along the Pittwater Road from Manly to Newport during the past two years was nearly 2000 and the traffic showed an increase of 50 to 75 per cent per annum.

From 1906 coaches from Manly to Bayview and Newport were operated by Coopers of Manly, who also hired out horses and traps. The same year the first motor omnibus commenced operations from Manly to Newport. A new improved service began in 1911 and naturally attracted holidaymakers but the rough road damaged wheels. During World War I two companies, Bottles Motor Service and The Diggers Pittwater Motor Company, operated from Narrabeen to Newport.

The electric tram line from Manly was gradually extended until it reached Narrabeen in 1913. It was known as the Pacific Loop. It was a single track with a passing bay. The trams bore distinctive destination symbols and the Narrabeen tram carried 'a black and white sign quartered diagonally with the white forming the ground work.' During his 1922 visit to Australia D H Lawrence took the tram to Narrabeen and swam naked in the Pacific.

In the 1920s Pittwater Road was called Victoria Street and across the road from the tram shed, now the Tramshed Community Centre, was Earley's Café, on the corner of Waterloo Street. The tram from Manly took 37 minutes to Narrabeen terminus. In the 1940s Bryson's Fish Shop stood on the site of Earley's Café, and the lakes could still be explored in a hired row boat up to the quiet waters of Deep Creek. In 1939 the tram ceased and the bus service from Wynyard to Palm Beach commenced. The red and yellow two storey buses wound their way out past Pittwater to Palm Beach. From the early 1950s many Sydney tram services were replaced with buses.

ABOVE: Family group and car outing to Palm Beach 9 June 1929. (H S Wyong, Pittwater Library Local Studies)

BELOW: The tram's passengers change at the Narrabeen terminus to catch a bus to Pittwater in c1917. (Vic Solomons)

AVALON
'The centre of the most beautiful district around Sydney'

THE A J Small advertisement for the private sale of the Avalon Beach Estate in 1930 read 'The centre of the most beautiful district around Sydney'. A J Small and his family first visited the area late in 1912. They stayed at a house named The Owl, when they came for holidays, which was owned by the Scarrs and stood opposite where Paradise Beach Road leaves Riverview Road. Small built a home, which also served as an office, in Bellevue Avenue on his first land subdivision in 1920. The name Avalon was not in use until late 1921. His brochure and plan for the auction sale of the Palmgrove Estate in December 1921 shows 'Avalon Beach'. Mrs Muriel Hunt, nee Small, in 1985 said her father woke her mother one night to tell her of his inspiration to name the area. He had in mind the Avalon of Celtic mythology. Soon afterwards Small erected a signboard on the top of Bilgola Hill that read 'Behold the Vale of Avalon – Tennyson'.

From 1824 Father John Joseph Therry (1790–1854) was promised and granted land on the peninsula. Therry, who arrived on the *Janus* in 1820, was the first official Catholic priest in the colony. Avalon was part of his 1833 grant of 1200 acres made by Governor Bourke. A portion of the area was once known as Priest's Flat. In the 1860s the natural phenomena, the Hole in the Wall, a stone arch which collapsed in a gale in 1867, and St Michael's Cave, attracted tourists, some walking from Palm Beach to Avalon Beach.

By the 1920s Avalon's natural beauty attracted many people at Christmas and holiday periods and tents and lean-tos provided shelter. Small promoted the area as a place of pleasure and capitalised on a building boom. In the 1930s Small established the Avalon Private Picnic and Camping Grounds. He built a general store in 1921–1922 at the junction of Barrenjoey Road and Avalon Parade. The first tenant was a Newport man named Snape. In 1926 the store was extended with a tearoom and later a luncheon room. Amongst later tenants were Stan Wickham, who had been an 1890s rugby union player, Mrs Ralph, and in the 1950s le Clercq. In 1960 the store was sold to Ezra Norton and subsequently demolished for new premises, including the Barefoot Boulevarde. Stan Wickham built his own store opposite Small's property and here in 1933 the first post office opened. This store was later operated by Mrs Wickham's nephew, Bill McDonald. At North Avalon, near the intersection of Barrenjoey and Careel Head Roads there was the Hammond Dairy, with 110 cows. Milk was delivered locally by horse and cart. The Hammond children made pets of koalas living in the trees around the dairy.

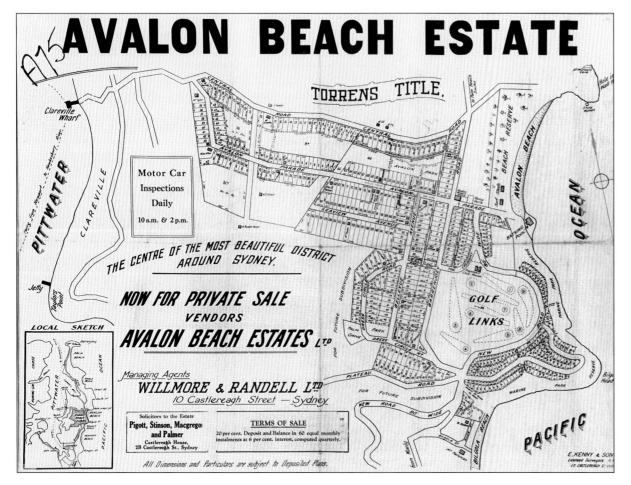

LEFT: Originally a weekend and holiday retreat, A J Small first offered the Palmgrove Estate for sale on 26 December 1921. In the 1930s more permanent settlers bought property. By the 1950s Avalon was still seen as a village. Avalon Beach Estate was auctioned in 1930. (Warringah Library Local Studies)

OPPOSITE: Avalon Beach of the 1940s with distant sandhills in view. (Warringah Library Local Studies)

Small was president of both the New South Wales Town Planning Association and the Parks and Playgrounds movement. He was a councillor of the Millions Club, which encouraged British migration to make Sydney the first Australian city to reach a population of one million.

Small's city office was close to Ruskin Rowe's, who served on the Town Planning Association Council. Rowe was the son of the noted architect, Thomas Rowe, the first mayor of Manly. Rowe also had a weekender, The Cabbage Trees, at Avalon. The district was rustic with rough tracks for roads, fish and eels in the creek and numerous native animals, including koalas. Another architect attracted to the area was A S Jolly, who arrived in the 1920s and joined an estate agent, A E Dalwood, to sell land. Jolly designed Careel House above Whale Beach in 1931 and the nearby Loggan Rock. In 1934 Jolly designed The Gem, later Hy-Brasil, high above Pittwater, for dentist Arthur Wilson. Artist Ted Herman later created the garden with sandstone walls and stairs where his daughter, artist Nada Herman Witkamp, captures the local bush and beach scenes in her oil paintings.

Since 1981 Hy-Brasil has had a permanent conservation order. Ruskin Rowe's teacher in architecture was Professor John Sulman and when Walter Burley Griffin came to Australia to work on Canberra in 1914 he found a kindred spirit in Sulman. At Avalon, Griffin designed Burley Griffin Lodge, between Plateau and Palmgrove Roads in 1935 for Miss Estelle James. The sandstone house, slightly enlarged in the 1960s by Sidney Ancher, was described by the National Trust of Australia (NSW) as 'the finest surviving example of a small house by Griffin'.

ABOVE: Enjoying the waters of the rock pool at Avalon, 1918. (Warringah Library Local Studies)

LEFT: Avalon car park in the late 1920s or early 1930s. The cars are covered for camping at the beach. (Warringah Library Local Studies)

Griffin and Small were councillors of the Wild Life Preservation Society. Together with people like David Stead, Thistle Y Harris, Bib and Bub creator, May Gibbs and the remarkable Marie Byles, the State's first woman solicitor, the society purchased land for £364 19s 7d to preserve a huge stand of angophora or Sydney red gum, reputedly 'discovered' by Small, and to protect koalas. The Angophora Reserve opened in 1938 and incorporates Hudson Park. It was listed on the Australian Heritage Commission Register of the National Estate in 1989. It is a significant Aboriginal site, a refuge for surviving koalas and represents a quiet memory of Avalon's original bushland.

By the 1940s the area attracted a bohemian community where artists like Arthur Murch, Sali Herman, sculptor Bonar Dunlop, Margaret Jay from Sydney's Rowe Street and visiting friends such as William Dobell and Hal Missingham talked and worked. In the 1950s the Avalon Evening College commenced art classes and the art colony thrived. Artist Elaine Haxton lived locally as did well-known writer of the time Frank Clune and his wife, Thelma, who had a Sydney gallery and built a weekender in Ruskin Rowe.

The early houses of Avalon were mostly weekenders constructed of fibro and wood with fibro or iron roofs. It was not until after World War II that people began residing permanently in the suburb. Improved transport and the availability of cars increased its popularity. Avalon has a relaxed holiday atmosphere with many tropical plants thriving in local gardens. In the late 1990s locals were abuzz as the USA television 'soapie' *Baywatch* arrived to film on Avalon Beach. They planned to relocate to Sydney but complaints from residents forced them to opt for Hawaii.

ABOVE: Avalon Village, c1927 with the Avalon Beach Store to the left and a hoarding of Stapleton's estate agency on the right. (Warringah Library Local Studies)

RIGHT: Plenty of boiling water is available for campers and picnickers at The Avalon kiosk in 1932. (Warringah Library Local Studies)

Avalon Beach

ABOVE AND OPPOSITE: Avalon Beach and the northern headland above in 1946, ' … those rocky bushland plateaus overlooking clefted cliffs, rolling surf, and beaches oddly fringed with Norfolk Pine … ' is how Ruth McTavish Drobnak described Avalon. A couple of houses cluster on the southern headland in the view opposite. (Warringah Library Local Studies)

Avalon Beach

Avalon Open Air Theatre

In the 1940s a tent theatre operated at weekends in Avalon on the site of the present cinema. Designed by architect Bruce Furse, a new theatre opened in August 1955. Built at a cost of £50 000, it was operated by Harold Spry and then his son Arnold and his wife Joan. The foyer was 'gaily coloured' and 'streamlined' and in keeping with the time the curtains featured Aboriginal motifs. In 1985 the cinema was sold to Mike Walsh.

In August 1950 a primary school opened at Avalon in a double portable building but a second building was soon required. A suggestion was made for an open-air theatre and an auditorium was erected in the space between the two school buildings. A disused RAAF building was obtained and placed near the school buildings with space for a stage. It was two years before the school's Parents and Citizens Association opened the theatre with a seating capacity of 200. Some of the audience sat on 'gaily coloured garden seats'.

Initially the theatre was used by the Avalon Evening College Drama Group, then by visiting drama groups and Sydney theatre groups. It was later used for migrant English classes, art shows, ballet, films, and musical recitals. The theatre proved popular as Avalon was far away from theatre facilities and there was no suitable hall in the suburb. Residents were able to indulge their love of music, drama and art.

ABOVE: Avalon in 1952: writing of his arrival on the peninsula in 1953 Morris West said 'The sun and the sand and the surf were free. The food at the wayside stalls was cheap, the bush was full of firewood, the coastal waystations – Mona Vale, Newport, Avalon – were still villages.'
(Warringah Library Local Studies)

LEFT: This scene at Avalon in 1952 resembles an outback settlement. (Warringah Library Local Studies)

OPPOSITE: Frank Hurley photographed Avalon Beach and village c1960.
(National Library of Australia)

Avalon Golf Links

Barrenjoey Road snakes above Bilgola Head beside Avalon Golf Course. It was Arthur J Small who was instrumental in the foundation of the golf links. A private company, Avalon Golf Links Pty Ltd, was formed with Small as governing director and his four children as directors and shareholders. A family ledger records the purchase of Canty's, a large area on the eastern side of (Old) Barrenjoey Road. In 1924 work commenced clearing the site which covered some 35 acres and the links opened in 1926. It was designed by well-known professional golfer of the period, Dan Soutar. On the site of today's golf club a starters hut was built but later a larger building was constructed. The manager and greenkeeper for many years was Ted Hock, who was succeeded by C A Sanders. Later the clubhouse was extended to include a dining room.

A J Small died in 1953 and in 1956 the golf links were sold to Warringah Shire Council. In 1959 the golf links company went into voluntary liquidation. Sixteen subdivided residential blocks were excised from the golf links and were sold by the estate of the late A J Small. Picturesque Avalon Golf Links is a public course of 9 holes now operated by Pittwater Council.

LEFT: Avalon in 1978 with the remains of the original Avalon sandhills, top left. (Roads and Traffic Authority)

OPPOSITE ABOVE: Compare this 1960 view of Avalon with today's busy roads. (Roads and Traffic Authority)

OPPOSITE RIGHT: Avalon in 1960 and blissful days of scant traffic. (Roads and Traffic Authority)

BARRENJOEY

THE striking Barrenjoey Headland forms the southern entrance to Broken Bay and is washed by the Tasman Sea. The name means 'young kangaroo' but the land is shaped like a hammer head shark. Atop the rugged cliffs is the 1881 Barrenjoey Lighthouse.

On 16 March 1816 Governor Macquarie granted Surgeon James Napper 400 acres extending from Barrenjoey Headland to Whale Beach which Napper named Larkfield. It was acquired by D'Arcy Wentworth and later became part of the Bassett-Darley estate. In 1881 the government purchased 147 acres of Barrenjoey Headland and the spit for £1250.

In the early 1800s there were shipwrecks in the Broken Bay area as many vessels plied the Hawkesbury carrying produce to Sydney. In 1805 the population along the river was 2000. In addition there was the coastal traffic of cedar and coal from the Hunter River and later steamers travelling from the Macleay and Clarence Rivers. By the 1870s over 350 ships a year used the Hawkesbury River.

Both Broken Bay and Pittwater offered shelter during storms and gales. In 1855 a fire beacon was lit in a simple basket to assist mariners but by 1863 a Select Committee called for a lighthouse. In 1867 wild weather and floods washed away the gardens of the Chinese huts on Barrenjoey's sandy spit and Hawkesbury crops and household items littered the

ABOVE: The summit of the Barrenjoey headland with Barnet's lighthouse and adjacent buildings in view. Originally an oil burner light, it later converted to electricity and the light was seen for a distance of 50 kilometres.
(Humphrey Collection, National Library of Australia)

LEFT: Robert William Russell adjusting the kerosene burners on the lighthouse lamp in 1925.
(Manly, Warringah & Pittwater Historical Society)

The view looking north-east from Sunrise Hill to Lion Island, Barrenjoey Headland and Palm Beach, with only a few houses in sight, 1925. (NSW Government Printing Office)

beaches from Barrenjoey to Long Reef. The following year two temporary lights were provided on the inner south headland, known as Stewart's Lights or Towers. Stewart was the Member for East Sydney who, with others, raised the issue in the Legislative Assembly of the need for a light on the headland. Colonial Architect, James Barnet, was one of the officials who selected the site. George Mulhall became Superintendent of the Lights with his son George as assistant.

Barnet was selected as the architect for a lighthouse and the foundation stone was laid on 15 April 1880. Guests travelled from Circular Quay to Manly by ferry, rode a coach to Bayview and caught a steamer up to Barrenjoey. Barnet's daughter Rose laid the foundation stone. The light was first lit on 1 August 1881. The first lighthouse keeper George Mulhall Senior and his wife Mary are buried close to the lighthouse. In 1932 the Barrenjoey light became automatic.

From 1968 until 1997, when the reserve passed to the National Parks and Wildlife Service, Jervis Sparks and his wife Bridget lived in one of the assistant keepers' stone cottages. Sparks founded the Barranjoey (sic) Historical Resources Centre and published *Tales From Barrenjoey* and *The Red Light of Palm Beach*. The couple left the area in 1998 but Jervis Sparks contributed advice on the restoration of the Barrenjoey Lighthouse.

ABOVE: Campers at one of the semi-permanent cabins 'Duzme' at Governor Phillip Park camping area, Barrenjoey in the 1950s.
(J Coleman, Warringah Library Local Studies)

LEFT: The popular and ordered camping area at Governor Phillip Park, Barrenjoey, c1950.
(Mrs Bilton, Warringah Library Local Studies)

OPPOSITE: Tent city located in Governor Phillip Park was a favourite holiday location for many years. Pressure from locals and council closed the park in 1972.
(Warringah Library Local Studies)

The Customs Station

Smuggling was rife at Pittwater and a customs station was established 'in a comfortable little nook behind Barren Joel [sic]' in 1843. John B Howard was the first official appointed to control the illicit traffic of rum, brandy and tobacco. In 1861 Alexander T Ross and his wife entertained the Sydney coroner here. He appreciated the couple's 'hospitality, kindness and urbanity' and found the family had no illness while resident in the locality. Ross led the visitors to the headland to admire the views and they noted the strange life-size painted wooden soldiers, made from trees, used as landmarks for shipping.

By that time the customs station buildings had deteriorated beyond repair. The Colonial Architect gave a quote of £600 for the erection of new quarters for the customs officer and boatmen. In 1862 a stone Customs House, boatman's cottage, boathouse and stone jetty were built. The customs men rendered aid in times of disaster and in 1871 Mr Black, the then Customs Officer, and his crew rescued men from a three-ton open sailing vessel. The Customs House remained a place of refuge and comfort for survivors of misadventure. The first school was held in 1872 in the boatman's cottage, close to the customs station. In 1976 the customs station was destroyed by fire.

ABOVE: The woman golfer, Vera Russell, was the lighthouse keeper's daughter.
(Vera Russell, Warringah Library Local Studies)

LEFT: The house of Barney Horton in the 1920s. He was one of the founders of the Palm Beach Golf Club.
(Laurie Seaman)

OPPOSITE: An early view of the customs buildings at the foot of Barrenjoey, with the sand dunes. Nearby Chinese fishermen had a fish salting works and exported fish to China or sent it to the Chinese on the Victorian goldfields.
(National Library of Australia)

From the early 1900s campers enjoyed the beauty of the area and during the Depression semi-permanent dwellings appeared. Later generations stayed at the Warringah Shire Council's camping ground. In 1942 there were 70 campsites and 180 by 1955.

Part of the Lighthouse Reserve, which became Governor Phillip Park, was used for golf. In 1924 the Palm Beach Recreation Club Limited officially opened a golf course. Cattle wandered the course and it was rather wild. One golfer complained that a cow ate her ball. White painted stones marked the tees. In 1932 the course was fenced off. There were small dairies in the vicinity, one owned by George Hitchcock, the Warringah Shire Council president and a founding member of the Palm Beach Golf Club. His house, with some early boatsheds, was destroyed by a storm c1930. Another dairy was owned by the Gonsalves family. Midge Gonsalves was one of the best golfers at the club.

W M (Billy) Hughes was one of the first honorary members and often visited. Samuel Hood Hammond, father of opera singer Joan Hammond (1912–1996), was president in 1927. The Hammond weekend home Dormy was demolished to build the clubhouse on Beach Road. Overlooked by Barrenjoey Headland, Palm Beach Golf Course has magnificent views of Pittwater and Broken Bay. It is a 9 hole course leased from Pittwater Council.

The view in 1926 as it looked north along Station Beach to Barrenjoey Headland and the lighthouse. (NSW Government Printing Office)

BEAUTIFUL BAYVIEW

THE rugged heights of Bayview were thickly timbered until the casuarinas or forest oaks were plundered by early shingle getters and sold for high prices in Sydney. Robert McIntosh Senior and his wife and family arrived in the colony in 1814. McIntosh left the army and in 1817 Governor Macquarie promised him 200 acres at Pittwater (now Bayview). By 1819 he was a constable for the district and in the 1828 census McIntosh was resident at Pittwater. McIntosh died in 1829 and land promised to him was finally granted in 1833 by Governor Bourke. His eldest son Robert held an adjoining 40 acres next to the original grant. Robert Junior married Jane Pymble, daughter of North Shore pioneer, Robert Pymble, and the McIntosh family is closely associated with the history of Gordon. Jeremiah Bryant was also promised 80 acres in 1821, the last year of Macquarie's governorship but his Bayview land was also not granted until 1833.

In the early years of white settlement there were still Aborigines in the area and one resident recalled that as a young girl she saw a native spear a fish while standing under a mangrove tree. The settlers had self sufficient farms with orchards, vegetables and poultry. In 1867 one visiting clergyman found some residents had never been

A general view from Bayview in 1914. Many mangroves around Sydney were destroyed when land was reclaimed for development. (Warringah Library Local Studies)

to Sydney and declared them 'in a measure uncivilised'. Forests provided timber for boat building with ketches still being built in the 1870s. Around 1900 railway sleepers and bakers' wood were still being cut locally. In 1901, when the Bayview Wharf was built, mangroves lined the foreshores.

The Shaw Brothers, descendants of Joseph and Susan Shaw who arrived from Yorkshire in 1834, were local boat builders near Shaw's Creek. Originally the creek was wide enough for boats to pass along its length and it was a popular fishing spot. James Shaw, known as 'Old Jim Shaw the Blacksmith', ran his business in a shop at the corner of Pittwater and Cabbage Tree Roads. He was attached to an old Indian motorcycle which he rode until he was 75 years of age. The Indian was superseded by a Vespa motor scooter. Two of Shaw's vessels became pearling luggers in Darwin.

Around 1900 J Austin and James Symond operated a brick kiln and drying sheds on Taylor's Flat in Bayview Road to manufacture 'superior quality bricks'. In the late 1890s waterfront homes were built by P Taylor and Sir Rupert Clarke. Cape's Flat, named for the 40 acre grant to William Timothy Cape, headmaster of the 1834 Sydney College, was a popular picnic area. Nearby were orchards of oranges, peaches, nectarines and summer fruits. The Collins family, who had early associations with Pittwater, also made jams and preserves from their orchard produce. They owned an 80 acre farm, and a post office opened in the family home on 21 August 1882 when the name Bayview was adopted.

ABOVE: A distant view of Bayview House from Loftus Point, Newport, photographed by Henry King. Originally Lord Loftus Point named after the New South Wales Governor, it later became known as Green Point. (Warringah Library Local Studies)

LEFT: Mrs Edith Codrington operated a boarding house at Bayview in the early 1900s. Three of the guests are identified as members of the Reynolds family. (Mitchell Library, State Library of NSW)

Loquat Valley School

Bayview's Loquat Valley School was a portion of Robert McIntosh Senior's grant. The property was owned by P Taylor, then by his son, the aviator Sir Patrick Gordon Taylor (1896–1966) who flew with Sir Charles Kingsford Smith. Taylor had definite views on education and wanted children to learn about the peoples of the world, their culture and history. He also wanted children to have pride in and love for their country. The first classes were held on an enclosed veranda, with Mrs Gomme as headmistress. Taylor's daughters were two of the original 13 pupils. His daughter Gennie selected the school motto 'Aim High'.

In 1949 Mrs Day became headmistress and subsequently purchased the school but ill–health caused her to sell it in 1967 to the Sydney Church of England Girls' Grammar School which continued to operate it as Loquat Valley School. Mrs Millicent Prescott became headmistress. Many local children attended the delightfully situated school which is now called Loquat Valley Anglican Preparatory School.

ABOVE: Access to the peninsula was mostly by boat as Barrenjoey Road was very rough. People alighted here at Newport Wharf. Bayview is in the distance.
(Warringah Library Local Studies)

RIGHT: This early scene of Bayview is taken near Killarney Cottage and Baker's orchard in 1928.
(Mrs Moore, Warringah Library Local Studies)

Bayview Golf Club

Bayview Golf Course covers several early land grants including that of Peter Patullo who held land 'at North Harbour, opposite Scotland Island'. George McIntosh, son of Robert McIntosh Junior, held 43 acres at Winnererremy with Shaw's Creek and swamp, which the Lands Department later marked as Winni Jenny. The area is now named Winnererremy. Winji Jimmi had been given as the name of a small local reserve.

John Orr, a sheep farmer from Hawkes Bay in New Zealand visited Sydney in 1920 and purchased land at Bayview. He and his wife Christina built a house there in 1924. They enjoyed golf and created a six hole course for themselves. A punt was used to drag trees along and mount up the dirt to form fairways, filling in the existing swampland. The tide brought large amounts of salt water into the swamp twice daily and so Orr built flood gates where Pittwater Road crossed Shaw's Creek.

The Orr's were hospitable and friends joined them in

the game. They took rugs, picnicked and then returned to the Orr's home for billiards and ale. In 1926 a club was formed with a hut for a clubhouse. This was replaced in the 1930s with a small brick clubhouse. In 1933 the land was leased to H S Scott, a golf professional, and O F Clayton, both of Bayview. Christina Orr inherited the land upon the death of her husband in November 1941. Following World War II the Bayview Clubhouse was constituted and registered in 1948. Mrs Orr continued to reside in her original home

Looking north with Pittwater Road centre right and Bushrangers Hill top left on the horizon. (Warringah Library Local Studies)

but in 1967 the Bayview Golf Club purchased the whole property. The course is semi-private but non-members may play. Water features and clumps of cabbage tree palms make it an attractive course.

There is a significant culvert, constructed in 1951, near the Bayview Golf Course. Some elements of the culvert are of a later date. It crosses what is now a small tidal tributary to the south-western arm of Pittwater, just south of the junction of Pittwater and Cabbage Tree Roads. This watercourse was once part of the freshwater river rising from Winnererremy Swamp which covered most of the area now occupied by the golf course. Water drained into the swamp from the surrounding hills including the area called on early maps 'Cabbage Tree Flat'. It flowed into Pittwater through a meandering mangrove lined channel called the 'Newport Maze' on the eastern side of Pittwater Road. The maze vanished when the mangroves were bulldozed. The culvert dates from the post World War II period of road improvement and is an early example of pre-casting in concrete construction. The watercourse, though changed, is still part of the landscape with sluice gates fitted downstream, a reminder of the flood gates that John Orr built for his golf course. Close to Bayview Golf Course and bounded by Beaumont Crescent and Annam Road, Sir Edward Hallstrom had a private animal sanctuary. He had numerous birds, koalas and other animals, including nine albino kangaroos and two sets of white wallaby twins.

Looking north-east across Narrabeen Lagoon. The timber Ocean Road Bridge across the lagoon is partly submerged in flood water, c1900. (Warringah Library Local Studies)

Pittwater High School

In 1963 on a 'terribly wet' day Pittwater High School opened in an area reclaimed from mangrove swamp and filled with sand pumped from Winnererremy Bay. The headmaster, Mr Gorral, had a staff of ten full time and two part time teachers. Initially there were 220 pupils and on the first day only one building was completed and in the inclement weather it was necessary to walk on boards to classes. Three years later there were 974 pupils in 28 class groups, with a total staff of 45, including five subject masters. Unusually for a suburban school some 30 kilometres from Sydney, Pittwater High had an Agricultural Department. A well-appointed agricultural plot is maintained and students may study horticulture and animal husbandry.

Pittwater High was one of the first schools to offer surfing as a sport and also student driver education courses. In addition it is one of the few schools in Australia to own a yacht and offer sailing as a sport. This was introduced by Mr Vick in 1968. Local boat builders helped students build their own yacht *Kalori*. It was launched in 1970 at the Royal Prince Alfred Yacht Club by Lady Cutler, wife of the Governor of New South Wales, Sir Roden Cutler VC.

Pittwater High maintains a high standard in the performing arts and sports. Actor Tom Burlinson was school captain in 1983 and later trained at NIDA. In 2001 Pittwater High received an award for Excellence in the Performing Arts from the Director of Education.

The school has a cultural student exchange programme with its sister school in Wilmette, Chicago, New Trier High School. In addition the school has an exchange programme with a Japanese high school.

This innovative Bini Shell was erected as the Pittwater High School Auditorium. Unfortunately the dome of the shell collapsed on 5 August 1986 and a school cleaner was injured. A few days later when asbestos was discovered in the rubble there was a 'teacher walkout'. (Mrs V Carey, Warringah Library Local Studies)

Maybanke Anderson

Maybanke Anderson (1845–1927) was a remarkable woman. Her family migrated to Sydney from England in 1854. In 1867 she married Edward Wolstenholme with whom she had seven children. Four died in infancy. In 1884 her unemployed, alcoholic husband deserted her. She raised her three sons, opened a college for girls, did voluntary work and was the foundation president of the Womanhood Suffrage League of NSW in 1891, later becoming president. She was a social reformer, sex educator, feminist, suffragist and Federationist. Maybanke was also foundation president of the Kindergarten Union, opening their first free kindergarten in 1896. In 1892 she divorced the absent Wolstenholme. In 1899 she married Professor Francis Anderson, first Professor of Philosophy at the University of Sydney. They lived at Forest Lodge but purchased a large block of virgin bushland at Bayview. The couple built a sandstone house which had views of Scotland Island and Pittwater. The journey to Bayview entailed a tram to Circular Quay, ferry to Manly and coach to the Rock Lily Hotel at Mona Vale where they were collected by cart or car.

The Bayview property was for holidays and weekends and the Andersons created a small farm. John and Lizzie Oliver worked for them. Lizzie was 'a superb cook' and her husband organised driving, boating and fishing trips and told many stories of early Pittwater. This resulted in Maybanke researching and writing *The Story of Pittwater* which was published in a journal of the Royal Australian Historical Society in 1920. George and Shelagh Champion circulated a paper in 1996 noting corrections to the publication.

A granddaughter, Marjorie, recalled 'glorious holidays at Bayview'. An undated *Daily Telegraph* article recorded an interview with Maybanke and stated 'with all her many and varied outside interests, Mrs Anderson is essentially a domesticated woman. At her home at Pittwater she forms a garden, knits and cooks, and enjoys the work which she thinks is especially the privilege of women'. The Andersons grew vegetables

A sewing group c1910, showing Maybanke Anderson fifth from the left in the middle row. (Pittwater Library Local Studies)

and roses and kept chickens and cows. On one occasion the professor, engrossed in a book while grazing a cow, had it fall over a cliff and break its neck. Maybanke also spent time writing. They kept 'open house' with parties in the house and grounds and years later university students recalled those happy occasions, with 'speeches, glorious food, coffee and cigars'.

Later the Andersons lived at Hunters Hill and from there undertook a European tour. Maybanke became ill and died in a hospital outside Paris in 1927. Her grave site is unknown.

Jorn Utzon and Bayview

In 1957 Danish architect, Jorn Utzon learned his design had won the international design competition for the Sydney Opera House. Utzon's father was a naval architect and Jorn Utzon studied Bennelong Point from nautical charts bought in Copenhagen. He understood the Opera House would be seen from all perspectives. He created an iconic building of the twentieth century. In 1963 Utzon brought his wife and three children to Sydney where he purchased land at Bayview and settled the family. He had a studio in a Palm Beach boat shed. His daughter Lin later declared the family 'adored Australia'. Pittwater, the yachts and boating life had similarities with the Danish life. Lin claimed Australia 'was a huge influence on all our lives' and she retained the strongest ties with the country, keeping in touch with friends and visiting Sydney. Utzon was forced to leave his uncompleted project in 1966, a tragedy both for him and the building.

With the decision to refurbish the Opera House using technological advances, an approach was made to Utzon for his input. His son Jan, who commenced studies in architecture in Sydney, has assisted with translation of his father's ideas into detailed drawings. Utzon has never seen the completed Opera House.

Jorn Utzon discusses plans for the future Opera House on the site of the Fort Macquarie tramsheds on 29 July 1957. (Ken Renshaw, Mitchell Library, State Library of NSW)

Dame Nellie Melba outside the first Bilgola House c1905 which was built by the Hon. William Bede Dalley in 1870. This house was replaced by a grander home in 1919. (Allen Album, Mitchell Library, State Library of NSW)

BELGOULA – BELGOOLA – BILGOLA

IN 1815 Irish emancipist surveyor James Meehan recorded the name 'Belgoula'. In 1822 Robert Henderson, involved in smuggling brandy and rum at Pittwater, was granted 100 acres that he named 'Belgoola' or 'Belgooler'. Today's spelling derives from Bilgola House built by state parliamentarian, William Bede Dalley in the 1870s when he acquired land from the Therry estate.

Father Therry explored for coal around Bilgola Head and in 1859 when the Sydney Coroner J S Parker visited Broken Bay he stated he found 'coal cropping out of the mountain' on the Therry property. Parker believed coal would be a future important export. There was also a shaft on Avalon Golf Links.

In 1862 the Therry residence on the farm was destroyed by fire, later found to have been 'wilfully and maliciously' started by an unknown person. The same year the property was taken up by distant relatives of Father Therry's, James Therry of Waterford in Ireland and his wife Maria.

A romantic 1914 view of an isolated Bilgola House with the beach fenced off from the home. (Warringah Library Local Studies)

Colonel Walter Oswald Watt, an officer in the French Air Force in 1914, purchased the Bilgola home. He was awarded the Legion of Honour and the Croix de Guerre. He joined the Royal Flying Corps in Britain and commanded the Australian No. 2 Squadron in 1917. Watt accidentally drowned in 1921 at Bilgola Beach.

The cottage at Bilgola was then demolished and a weekend home built on the site by Sydney businesswoman, Mrs Maclurcan. The property was described in *The Garden Magazine* on 1 December 1926 as a beautiful dream home which stood 'snugly amongst a particularly fine grove of well developed native palms in the most thickly wooded portion of Bilgola Beach'.

ABOVE: A tricky manoeuvre by contractor Mervyn Farley who built the Serpentine Road at Bilgola Head with this adaptable machine. He was photographed by Milton Kent in 1928. (Mervyn and Gretchen Farley)

LEFT: Bilgola House in the 1940s enjoyed an idyllic position close to the sea set amongst the local cabbage tree palms. The secluded beach is classified as dangerous. (Warringah Library Local Studies)

CAREEL BAY

IN 1792 Lieutenant William Dawes, whilst on an excursion to Barrenjoey, noted the land above Careel Bay as good pasture for sheep. The name Careel Bay is recorded in the Grant Register of 1816 but when Captain F W Sidney surveyed Pittwater between 1868 and 1872 he noted the bay on his chart as Evening Bay, with the southern entrance marked as Stripe Bay.

In 1832, according to the *New South Wales Calendar*, there were two small farms and cottages. In 1837 Father J J Therry acquired 280 acres adjoining his 1833 grant of 1200 acres. His land covered Bilgola Head to Saltpan Cove and north to Careel Bay. This latter grant was an exchange for land at Parramatta and Therry named it Mount Patrick. Therry built a small wooden church at Careel Bay, the site near today's Patrick and Therry Streets Avalon and planned a settlement to be named Josephton. The church was later moved to Narrabeen.

In 1861 when Charles de Boos travelled on horseback from Manly to Barrenjoey, he visited the farm of John and Honora Collins at Careel Bay. He found the small homestead whitewashed and neat and the atmosphere pretty and picturesque. The earthern floor of the farmhouse was spotless, the tinware shone like silver and de Boos thought it the 'very beau ideal of cleanliness'. Dawes was correct in his assumption of the area being good pasture for Collins grew wheat and kept a dairy, and Mrs Collins sent produce to Sydney. In 1878 a provisional school operated at the Collins homestead.

When Therry died, the Maritime Village of Brighton (Josephton) was surveyed by Hallen and McEvoy. In 1871 streets were marked out, a wharf for steamers planned and 112 building lots pegged out between the water and bushland. On 3 May 1880 the Pittwater Estate was available at a city auction and block 3 at Clareville was sold to Sydney real estate agents, G Crowley and J M Taylor. Fifty acres were sold in 1915 near Avalon Parade and Clareville and in 1921 a further 39 acres was sold.

The long tradition of boat building still operates at Careel Bay. Charles Swancott claims a man named Bradbury built the first boats in the bay and there was early boat building activity at Stokes or Stripe Point.

Local boatmen and a few houses are the only intrusion in an area of heavily timbered hills at Careel Bay at the end of the nineteenth century. (Peter Verrills)

CHURCH POINT

ABOVE Church Point Wharf, amongst the spotted gums, is a tiny pioneer cemetery. This was the site of a small wooden Methodist church that gave the area its name of Chapel Point, changed to Church Point by 1888. Earlier pioneers George McIntosh and W H McKeown conducted services under a tree at Bayview until settler William Oliver sold an acre of land for ten shillings for the erection of the church. Settlers came by foot, horse or water to worship at the chapel built in 1872 with timber from Duffy's Forest, and a steep roof and tiny belfry. For four years from 1884 the building also served as Pittwater Public School and in 1887 Sir Henry Parkes, Member for St Leonards, visited the school. Parkes was the member for this area a number of times The first school master, Samuel Morrison missed the coach at Manly and walked towards Pittwater. Around Narrabeen John Collins gave him a lift, then rowed him to Bayview where he walked to the school. In 1888 a brick school was built near Bayview and Morrison lived nearby. In 1932 the church was demolished but the weathered headstones remain on the graves of early residents, including William Oliver.

William Oliver was born at Parramatta in 1805 and in 1822 was employed at Fiddens Wharf (Killara) on the Lane Cove River. He was a bailiff in 1830 when he married Mary Brown and was later employed as a policeman. By 1836 he was landlord of the Sawyers Arms and in 1842 Oliver and his wife operated a bakery. The Oliver's association with Pittwater began in 1838 when William purchased 50 acres at The Basin. He realised the potential of the stands of forest oak at

ABOVE: Travellers 'take a break' and pose on the dusty road at Church Point, c1910. (Warringah Library Local Studies)

BELOW: Church Point Wharf and store c1964. (Warringah Library Local Studies)

There is little activity at Church Point Wharf and General Store, 1920. J N S Wheeler wrote 'Boats, skiffs and a launch all huddled together at the wharf, waited to take visitors to their destinations. The lamp in the old store threw a glimmer on the road; the kerosene lamp on the post helped with the illumination. Bags filled with provisions were packed in the stern sheets and made all snug. Then the boats were rowed away. The tide came lapping along the rocky shore where the moonbeams dappled... ' (Warringah Library Local Studies)

A 1914 rural view of Church Point, complete with a lone cow. (Warringah Library Local Studies)

Pittwater for use in bakers' ovens and acquired land at Elvina Bay in 1842 and Lovett Bay 1858. He received 66 acres in 1864 at McCarrs Creek, which included most of Church Point to Ingleside.

At Pittwater the Olivers built some vessels including their lugger, *Thomas and Martha*. They owned *Bringa*, built in 1910 of oregon, with a tallowwood deck and copper-sheathed hull, and operated it as a timber tug, barge and crane.

The early wharf was less than a metre wide. It was replaced in 1885 with one wide enough to take a cart. It was upgraded in 1905. The wharf has always provided water access to Scotland Island and the western settlements.

Fishing, camping and pleasure excursions set out from the wharf. On McCarrs Creek, the inlet Brown's Bay was named for George Brown, who held 41 acres from 1880, named Waterside. In the early 1900s his farm was reached by track from Church Point and there were peach trees and passionfruit vines in the garden. The area was fertile and grapes grew at Church Point and watermelons at Bayview. Near the track, which became

ABOVE: McCarrs Creek Pittwater photographed by William Henry Broadhurst. Broadhurst was a commercial photographer who travelled widely in New South Wales in the early twentieth century. His more than 1100 hand coloured postcards provided a detailed record of Sydney suburbs and coastal areas of the State. (Mitchell Library, State Library of NSW)

RIGHT: In 1907 a track was made from McCarr's Creek through the thickly wooded bush to Coal and Candle Creek by James Booth. It was commonly called Booth's Track. The obelisk was erected in 1943 by the Manly, Warringah & Pittwater Historical Society to commemorate surveys of McCarr's Creek in 1789 by Captain John Hunter, in 1829 by William Govett and in 1868 by Captain F W Sidney of the Royal Navy. (Mitchell Library, State Library of NSW)

Quarter Sessions Road, was Simpson's fruit orchard and a bountiful flower garden. Melrose, built in 1888, operated as a boarding house for some years. On 1 January 1909 a post receiving office opened at the store of James Booth. On 15 May 1912 a new post office opened. From the 1920s the Pasadena became a local landmark built on the site of Booth's store. The two storey building with a veranda facing the roadway was operated by C F Wymark and included a store and residence. The Pasadena had a succession of owners and survives as a small motel beside Pittwater.

ABOVE: Brown's Bay in 1928. Stone steps led to a jetty in the bay from where a track led to Dorothy's Bower, named for a member of the Brown family.
(Warringah Library Local Studies)

LEFT: Brown's Point, Church Point, as it was in 1947. The bay was named after Brown's Estate, where the Brown family lived in a weatherboard cottage. The area was thick with flannel flowers. (Warringah Library Local Studies)

OPPOSITE: A steam ferry approaches Clareville Wharf, Pittwater, c1910. (Warringah Library Local Studies)

CLAREVILLE

CLAREVILLE was a portion of Father Therry's grants and Stokes Point recalls James Stokes, who lived on the southern arm of Careel Bay in 1833 and 1841. Reputedly a London shoemaker transported for stealing, he began shipbuilding on the point and lived alone in the area in the 1850s. Thomas Warner later held 50 acres on the point, which was acquired by George Green, who sold to John Collins in 1870. J Taylor had 30 acres at Taylor's Point.

At one time, when Arthur Small was buying land, the ocean beach at Avalon was known as Clareville. By the 1920s this tranquil spot was subdivided and holiday homes built in the bushland. Described as a paradise with native flora and fauna, including koalas, oysters on the rocks and good fishing, the holiday life was basic with tank water, no electricity, fuel camp ovens and the danger of bushfires. There was a regular boat service from Hawkesbury River Station to Clareville Wharf. In the 1930s artist Robert Johnson built a house of local sandstone at Clareville and later another artist Frank Hodgkinson and wife Val, part of the Avalon art community, lived at Clareville. One of his works is in the foyer of the Westin Hotel (formerly the GPO) in Sydney. By the 1950s Clareville became a residential area but with the summer drone of cicadas and the lushness of flowering hibiscus and frangipani Clareville retains something of its remoteness from the city.

Ross Estate, Clareville, Pittwater

How Values Must Rise

Because the population of Sydney has more than doubled itself since 1900, and that two-fifths of our entire population are crowded into an area less than 7,000 acres in the congested suburbs, the result is that the demand for land at the seaside resorts more than doubly increases each year, and each year has been a silent witness of the wisdom of investing in seaside land. This is just the reason why you should get in early before the prices are prohibitive.

Commodities

A large General Store has been erected near the beach, where all household commodities can be obtained. Also afternoon teas and refreshments are provided in first-class style.

Meat, milk, butter and eggs are delivered, and so those with week-end homes here find every necessity provided for them.

The Magnificent **PALM GLEN** which has been dedicated as a Park is close to the Estate and is indeed one of the show places of the district, and makes a lovely cool picnic ground.

FOR PRIVATE SALE BY . . . Norman Gill 117 PITT STREET, SYDNEY and Walker & Mount Sts., North Sydney

Telephones: City 10867. North 1212.

PITTWATER

Pittwater has long ago earned for itself the name of Killarney on account of its beauty. Its fine stretch of water undulating Hills, Bays and Beaches make it a rival to many of the most beautiful Harbours in the World.

It is fast becoming the sailing ground of New South Wales. The Prince Alfred Yacht Club has purchased a large area of ground on one of its foremost points for a Club House Site and Rendezvous for its members whilst annually a local Regatta is held. Every Easter a large number of Yachts find their way to Pittwater.

There are regular services of Motor Launches running daily from Newport to all the Wharfs including Clareville Wharf (which is 5 minutes from Estate) as far as Palm Beach, whilst a regular service is run from the Hawkesbury Railway Station to all the Wharfs to Newport.

What the future of this beautiful Harbour is to be is easily imagined.

ROSS ESTATE, Clareville, Pittwater
For Private Sale by NORMAN GILL,
117 Pitt Street, Sydney, and Walker and Mount Sts, North Sydney

ROSS ESTATE
CLAREVILLE PITTWATER

THE BATHING POOL AT AVALON BEACH

ROSS ESTATE, CLAREVILLE, PITTWATER

THE ESTATE is only 14 miles from Manly, and is between Pittwater and Avalon Beach. It has glorious views of both, and has the advantage of being easily accessible to either. There are two routes to choose from to get there, one is by Motor Bus from Narrabeen Tram Terminus to Newport, thence by fast Launch to Clareville Wharf, which is only three minutes from the Estate, or by Direct Motor Bus to Avalon Parade, which runs off Main Barrenjoey Road, and is within 10 minutes easy walk to the Estate.

SCENERY.—All along the road, right to the Estate, glorious panorama views are obtained, and each turn of the road opens up a fresh surprise of glorious bursts of grand Coastal and Water Scenery, and both routes are so beautiful that words are too feeble to convey the emotions of an appreciative observer.

Our Fleet of Cars

Our Cars are available to intending purchasers free of charge to view the Estate, and we feel confident that those who choose to view the Estate will find that we have not over stated our remarks about this property.

Surfing and Bathing

The Beach (which is the next Beach north of Bilgola) is within easy walking distance of this beautiful and elevated Estate and offers excellent surfing facilities and every convenience in the way of Dressing Sheds. Lifelines for safety have been provided.

Another feature is the Large Bathing Pool cut out of the Solid Rock, right at the beach (southern end). It is extremely popular with Women and Children, to whom the absolute safety appeals. It is also well patronised by men, being so near the Surfing Beach. A Ladies' Dressing Shed has been built at the pool.

Fishing

To make Fishing an enjoyable sport the fish want to be plentiful. The Harbour (Pittwater) is famous for its fine fishing grounds, the fish being of great variety, and plentiful, while the Ocean Beach and Rocks have indeed earned a good name for their fishermen, who can always rely on getting something good and choice. The fishermen say that the fish are always hungry here, and are the right sort to catch.

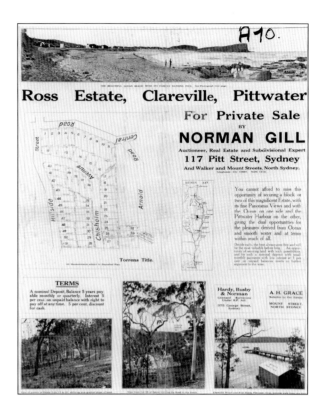

A10.

Ross Estate, Clareville, Pittwater

For Private Sale
BY
NORMAN GILL

Auctioneer, Real Estate and Subdivisional Expert
117 Pitt Street, Sydney
And Walker and Mount Streets, North Sydney.

You cannot afford to miss this opportunity of securing a block or two of this magnificent Estate, with its fine Panorama Views and with the Ocean on one side and the Pittwater Harbour on the other, giving the dual opportunities for the pleasures derived from Ocean and smooth water and at terms within reach of all.

Decide early, the best always goes first and well for the most valuable before long. An opportunity of securing land with such possibilities, and for such a nominal deposit with small monthly payments with low interest at 5 per cent. on unpaid balances seems too barren argument to lose now.

Torrens Title.

TERMS

A nominal Deposit, Balance 5 years payable monthly or quarterly. Interest 5 per cent. on unpaid balance with right to pay off at any time. 5 per cent. discount for cash.

Hardy, Busby & Norman
A. H. GRACE

ABOVE: Clareville's Ross Estate for sale. Note the photographs of two lots and the Clareville Wharf and boat shed 'three minutes walk from the estate'.
(Warringah Library Local Studies)

LEFT: Clareville for sale! The area was subdivided in the 1920s, mostly for holiday homes. Note the illustration of the car 'available for intending purchasers free of charge to view the Estate'. Intending purchasers were informed a 'large General Store has been erected near the beach, where all household commodities can be obtained'.
(Warringah Library Local Studies)

ELANORA HEIGHTS

GOVERNOR Phillip sighted the land above Narrabeen Lakes in 1788. Botanist George Caley walked from today's West Pennant Hills on a journey to the sea in February 1805. Feverish and ill he saw the lakes and passed around the north side which he named Cabbage Tree Lagoon. Elanora is an Aboriginal name thought to mean 'camp by the sea'. A portion of the area was once known as Green Hills.

Grants were made in 1810 and a few small farms developed. In 1888 a drill was sunk near Deep Creek and 27 metres down a bed of fossil oyster shells was discovered. The drilling continued and at 370 metres natural gas was found which, through lead pipes, was piped to a local cottage for lighting and a stove. At 580 metres a seam of non-bituminous coal was discovered but following consultation with Professor Edgeware David the drilling was abandoned.

In the 1920s Land Properties and Investment Ltd purchased a large area of land that was named the Elanora Heights Estate, described as 'The Bellevue Hill of the North'. With subdivision, the land was offered for sale on 9 March 1929. The Sydney Harbour Bridge was being constructed and it was felt the bridge would give easier access to the area, some 20 kilometres from Sydney. It was decided that a golf course would attract people to the region and in 1928 a committee formed with Brigadier T A J Playfair as chairman.

Some 165 acres of land was purchased in what was still a bush area and the Elanora Country Club formed

Warringah Shire Council at work in Elanora Heights in the 1940s. Ruth Park recalled the young Yorkshire botanist who 'floundered through here [Elanora] in the heat-sodden February of 1805. He felt "weak and faint, and was very hot, and it was a long time before I gave over sweating. Mosquettos troublesome" '.
(Warringah Library Local Studies)

in 1929. Playfair was president of the club from 1928–1965. The clubhouse was Kersaint House, which earlier had been a convalescent home for alcoholics. In 1937 this wooden building was destroyed by fire. The new clubhouse opened in 1938. In the 1950s the golf club's dam was an attraction for local boys. A bowling green opened in 1960. The Waterhouse family were club members. G A (Athol) born 1877 was an entomologist, E G (Gowrie) born 1881 and Professor of German at the University of Sydney, was a camellia expert. His former home Eryldene, in Gordon, is open to the public. L V L (Leslie), born 1886 was a mining engineer.

Today the 18 hole course, with its bushland setting and ocean views has tennis courts, a barbeque and children's play area. The club offers accommodation for

Kersaint was an old weatherboard building that served as the clubhouse for Elanora Country Club until 1937 when it was destroyed by fire. (Elanora)

affiliated members. Terry Smith, a member of the club, was awarded the Australian Sports Medal for services to golf writing in 2000. He has written some 15 books on golf and is considered 'the foremost expert on the history of the golf game in this country'. During the Depression some of the local men augmented the government 'dole' by caddying at the club, or finding and selling lost golf balls.

By the 1920s there were willows and clumps of wild arum lilies. A butcher sold meat to local households. There were no footpaths and Powderworks Road was known as Kabada Road. The Chappels owned a timber grocery shop and the Palmers ran a general store that was also the local post office. Children attended school at the Welfare Hall, which later became Bambach's Wireworks, until the North Narrabeen School was established. In periods of heavy rain Mullet Creek flooded the schoolyard. The Elanora Heights School opened in 1960. From their elevated position locals witnessed Narrabeen floods in 1927, 1942 and the late 1960s. In 1929 the Roxy Cinema opened in a hall in Waterloo Street, Narrabeen, and residents of Elanora Heights could enjoy a night at the 'flicks'. It had several changes of name, including the Odeon in 1955, but closed in 1959 to be replaced with shops.

Following World War II, improved transport and rising population meant the suburb gradually became a maze of streets and houses, the former bearing many Aboriginal names. It retains a bush atmosphere with Lumeah Reserve, Alleyne Lookout and Woorarra Lookout Reserve offering views of Narrabeen Lakes.

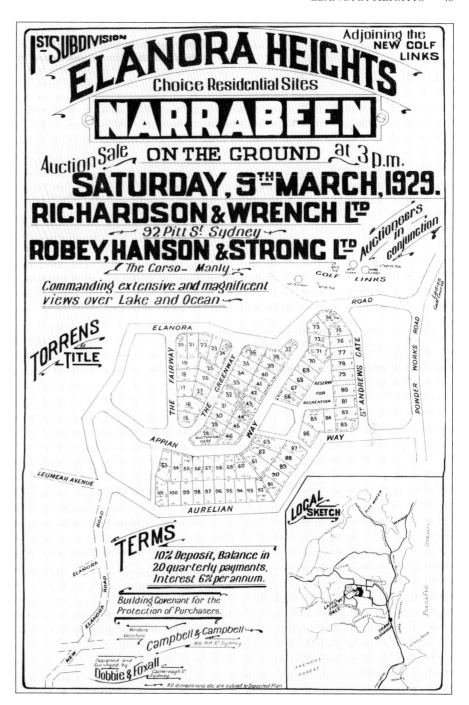

The original land sale on March 9 1929 for Elanora Heights. (Elanora)

INGLESIDE

T HE word 'ingle' derives from Scots Gaelic 'aingeal' meaning 'light', and came to mean a domestic fire or fireplace. Inglenook means 'the space on either side of a large fireplace'. Perhaps the charming name is unfortunate given the bushfires that have swept the area and kept the Ingleside Bush Fire Brigade in a state of constant vigilance.

In 1883 Carl von Bieren bought 320 acres on Sugar Loaf Hill from Robert Evans. Here the Dutch American, born in New York in 1844, built Ingleside House, a 13 room timber home with an ornate octagonal tower. Von Bieren claimed to have attended the University of Heidelberg and had two years in the School of Mines, Friedberg. He said he managed and then owned the Philadelphia Powder Company (known as Scranton's), which he sold in 1877. In the early 1880s he arrived in Sydney and the *Sydney Morning Herald* on 6 March that year stated a new industry was to be established at Narrabeen for the manufacture of blasting powder and gunpowder. 'It will be the only manufactory of the kind in the colonies'. A description was given of the site reached by 'a road passing through the properties of Messrs. Wheeler, Collins, Lick and Lawson'. The Inspector of Magazines checked the area and von Bieren was issued with a permit. He planned to purchase an additional 700 acres. At the head of a gully two magazines, 10 metres wide by 15 metres deep, were to be erected. Also planned were mixing, fine powder, charcoal, nitre, engine and clay houses together with a 4

ABOVE: Von Bieren's Powder Works at secluded Ingleside in 1885. The works became part of local legend. (Mitchell Library, State Library of NSW)

LEFT: A group photograph at the burnt shell of Ingleside House. It was destroyed in 1939. (Warringah Library Local Studies)

The Larkin family at Waratah Farm close to the junction of Powderworks Road and Mona Vale Road. The photograph was sent to Arthur Larkin in France in 1916 during World War I, entitled 'Grandma Larkin, Jock and Wid with lady friend A Hewitt'. (Warringah Library Local Studies)

metre square for the mixing of the explosive. Using natural springs he planned a 7000 gallon reservoir and employed quarrymen, stonemasons, carpenters and labourers to toil on the bush site. The Ingleside Powder Works was an ambitious scheme to manufacture all kinds of powders, from fine sporting, pellet and grain,

and a powerful blasting powder. Von Bieren also planned to make an explosive for torpedoes.

His company failed apparently because the government condemned the use of iron cylinders as dangerous when copper ones should have been used. He was tried and sentenced for embezzlement. When

Australia's first cowboy and country singer 'Smoky' Dawson with Steve Dodds and Smoky's sidekick 'Jingles' with two horses at his 'ranch' on Mona Vale Road 1 March 1968. (John Mulligan, National Library of Australia)

released after nine months in Goulburn Gaol, von Bieren became the proprietor of a sailors' boarding house in San Francisco. Many claimed von Bieren was an imposter but it was not until the outbreak of World War I that rumours he was a German spy started and all manner of tales circulated about the ruins in the bush.

Early in the twentieth century Florence and Isaac Larkin became caretakers of Ingleside House but it was destroyed by fire in 1939. A new Ingleside House rose at 42 Manor Road in Ingleside. The original stone gateposts were used, engraved with 'Advance Australia' over a depiction of a gun powder barrel.

The Larkins had an orchard at Narrabeen at the turn of the twentieth century and Arthur Larkin, with his horse and dray, worked on many local bridges and roads. Later they had another orchard, Waratah Farm, close to the junction of Powderworks Road (surveyed in 1885) and Mona Vale Road. It was here that Larkin propagated the Narrabeen Plum which became a popular variety. At the time the bush was full of native flora, including waratahs and boronia.

In 1951 the State government banned building on any lot less than two acres, so Ingleside has a rural atmosphere with a riding school, stables, firewood suppliers, landscape services, nurseries, a scout camp and 'Grandma's', a youth refuge, later named Warringah Youth Refuge. There were horse trails into Ku-ring-gai Chase National Park and their closure in 1987 was opposed locally.

For many years 'Smoky' Dawson's Ranch was on Mona Vale Road, close to Powderworks Road before it was destroyed by fire. 'Smoky' Dawson was born in 1913 in Melbourne and became famous as an Australian cowboy and a pioneer of Australian country music. He performed with his horse Flash and told stories, whip-cracked and threw axes and knives. He had a radio and television show and in 1978 was awarded the MBE. Always at his side is his wife Dot. In 2005 'Smoky' was inducted into the ARIA Hall of Fame.

Monash Country Club

The Monash Country Club was named for Lieutenant General Sir John Monash (1865–1931) Jewish lawyer and engineer. For his service during World War I Field Marshal Montgomery later wrote 'I would name Sir John Monash as the best general on the western front in Europe'. Monash Golf Club began as a Jewish social golf course because Jewish people were barred from many golf clubs in Sydney. Initially the participants played on a number of Sydney courses with a temporary small clubhouse at St Michael's Golf Course.

After World War II it was decided that the club would exclude no one and be open to all who wished to join regardless of creed, culture or colour. A property was selected at Ingleside but the area was very rough with thick bush, rock and swamp. In 1947 the Course Manager of the Elanora Country Club took on the challenge of building a championship course and three years later the 9 hole course was completed. A timber hut, purchased from the RAAF, served as a temporary clubhouse but was then partially destroyed by lightning. In 1951 the name changed from Monash Golf Club to Monash Country Club. Located 29 kilometres from Sydney, it was regarded as 'way out in the country somewhere'. A new clubhouse opened in 1952 only to be destroyed in a bushfire. A masonry dam was built to hold two and a half million gallons of water and a more luxurious clubhouse was built and opened by the Governor of NSW, Sir Eric Woodward.

Monash Country Club is a private golf course, although guests can accompany a member and it is described as 18 holes 'a fine full championship course, par 72'.

Lieutenant General Sir John Monash, Jewish lawyer and engineer for whom the Monash Country Club is named. (National Library of Australia)

The Baha'i Temple is a well-known landmark at Ingleside. Its height from the basement to the top of the spire is just under 40 metres. Following the 1979 revolution in Iran, the country of origin of the religion, the Australian Government defended the human rights of the Baha'is in Iran. From March 1982 a special humanitarian assistance programme enabled Iranian Baha'i refugees to migrate to Australia. The community has a long involvement in peace activities. The Baha'i Temple, with its high dome, is used by airliners and shipping for navigational purposes. (Warringah Library Local Studies)

The Baha'i Temple

From the early 1960s the Baha'i Temple has been a landmark on Mona Vale Road at Ingleside. The Baha'i faith came to Australia in 1920 with an English-Irish couple, Clara and Hyde Dunn. Hyde Dunn was a travelling salesman and as he worked he preached his faith, so small communities grew in different areas. By 1934 the National Spiritual Assembly of the Baha'i of Australia and New Zealand was established. In 1957 it was planned to build a Baha'i House of Worship in Sydney and 38 hectares at Ingleside, overlooking the Pacific Ocean, was chosen. The architect of the distinctive domed structure was John Brogan, of Sydney.

According to the faith, the nine sides and entrances represent the unity of the human race under one God, irrespective of ethnic and religious background. The Temple is one of only seven such structures in the world. The rotunda of the auditorium forms a regular nonagon, encircled by an inner ambulatory that in turn is encircled by an outer ambulatory, which serves as an entrance to the auditorium and connects the nine entrances to the temple.

The building of the temple used innovative construction techniques including a white quartz aggregate facing to the large exterior wall faces, set in special white cement. An additive allowed a delay in the setting of the concrete so it could be brushed to expose the quartz aggregates. A helicopter was used to raise the prefabricated lantern structure to the top of the completed dome of the building. It was the first time a helicopter had been used for building construction in Australia. Elements such as door and window frames, the segmented main arches with decorative concrete panels to the entrances, and the small domes over stairwells were prefabricated off-site to save time. At the base of the dome, a hollow ring girder was constructed to act as a reservoir for roof water collection. Construction began in April 1957 and took four years to complete at a cost of £150,000. On 17 September 1961 the Baha'i Temple was dedicated and opened to the public.

BONGIN-BONGIN TURIMETTA MONA VALE

IN the twenty first century Mona Vale is changing as town houses multiply and shopping areas expand. The Aborigines called it Bongin-Bongin. James Meehan surveyed the early farms. In 1814 Robert Campbell (1769–1846) became a land holder with 700 acres of very rich soil, well supplied with water even in the driest season. By the 1850s the name Mona Vale was in use, but in 1892 when the village was proclaimed it was called Turimetta. Mona Vale is said to be Celtic for 'high born'.

Campbell's land changed hands several times before the *Town and Country Journal* of 6 January 1877 found 'Narrabean and Mona Vale, Pitt Water' picturesque and interesting. After crossing the shallowest part of Narrabeen Lakes the visitor found Mona Vale 'secluded and quiet, and yet so grand, with the rugged ridges on the one hand, and the turbulent ocean on the other'. The journal claimed 'red-handed crime' had flourished and triumphed in the district.

Campbell's land was sold to Dr D'Arcy Wentworth, father of William Charles Wentworth. In the 1820s it was leased to emancipist, Martin Burke and farmed by David Foley. Foley constructed access up Foley's Hill and from 1842 for several years served as the Pittwater Constable. In 1858 Henry Bate and Frederick Berkelman leased land from Captain Darley, husband of Katherine Wentworth. Elizabeth Bate took her butter in a horse and cart to Manly Wharf where she shipped it for sale in Sydney. Their farm produced various crops including, potatoes, milk and pigs but they failed because of cattle duffing.

Mona Vale and Warriewood map; note Bongin Bongin Beach.
(Wilson's Street Directory 1931)

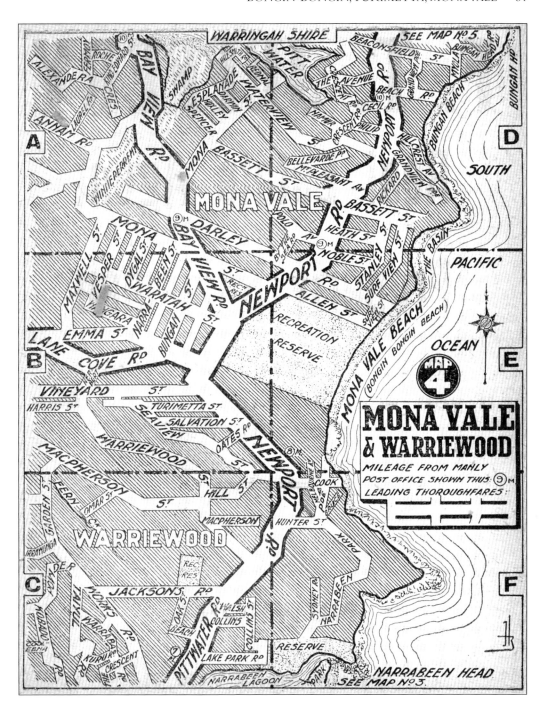

In 1860 the Mona Vale Estate was a rich agricultural and dairy farm, with clover grass, timber, and an abundance of pure water. In 1849 a murder resulted in locals, Thomas Collins and Francis Poyner, being apprehended. Poyner was found not guilty and Collins allowed to go free on recognizance, but to appear for murder if ever called. The next day Collins was charged with larceny. From 1849 to the 1870s family feuding, cattle and horse stealing, murder and accidental death occurred in the district. This turbulent time was known as 'the Mona Vale outrages'. In 1871 John Farrell III was sentenced to 3 years for cattle stealing, but served only two and a half years at Port Macquarie.

Those days were distant memories when land was auctioned in the early 1900s. A policeman had been established in 1899, in 1909 the constable was issued with a bicycle to cover his territory. Mona Vale was a small farming community in the early 1920s with roadside stalls. In 1928 the police station was still a one-man affair and the officer controlled from Mona Vale to Palm Beach and Pittwater. Weekend visitors ventured to Mona Vale and the peninsula, but there were drownings, sea rescues, and sometimes a shark attack. A joss house at Mona Vale was used by the local Chinese market gardeners. In the 1920s there were a few homes and holiday cottages and dirt roads. Reefs at the beach yielded many oysters, and fine snapper from the sea.

W Austin operated the general store and post office where locals purchased bread, butter, jam, candles and necessities. This sleepy lifestyle lasted until Mona Vale became more residential and commercial from the middle of the twentieth century.

ABOVE: A watercolour by H Brees of Boulton's Farm showing the distant Pittwater Church of England, 1860. (Mitchell Library, State Library of NSW)

LEFT: On the Pittwater Road just before the Bayview Golf Club c1960. (Roads and Traffic Authority)

There was still scattered settlement in Mona Vale in 1925. The Sydney Morning Herald in 1867 commented on the agrarian outrages of the district and the decay of the farms stating 'The history of the Mona Vale case reveals a condition of society, within a few miles of Sydney, that might well deter persons from settling there'. (Warringah Library Local Studies)

A memory of earlier times is the figure of a man and cart at the premises of E J Shaw & Son on Pittwater Road. A coloured man named Peter was employed by Mr Rundle, when he worked in Darwin, and drove Rundle's flat topped cart pulled by a water buffalo. In 1933 to attract passing trade on Pittwater Road, Rundle had a life size model made of Peter and his cart. It attracted more business to an adjacent stall, whose owner Noble purchased the model. It is now the trading symbol of E J Shaw & Son.

ABOVE: The first shops on Pittwater Road near the corner of Bungan Street housed the Mona Vale Post Office. The buildings were built by Steber Brothers and the hoardings advertise the newsagent, The Sun *newspaper and McNiven's Ice Cream, 1953. (Warringah Library Local Studies)*

LEFT: The corner butcher's shop at Mona Vale in 1934 stood opposite La Corniche.
(NSW Government Printing Office)

OPPOSITE: Mona Vale Beach c1960. (News Limited)

St John The Baptist and Dungarvon

St John the Baptist Anglican Church stands beside Pittwater Road and has a plaque that explains the church's many sites. A wooden church opened in 1871 on land donated by Captain Darley near the 'Eleven Mile Peg' (Bushrangers Hill). It was 11 miles from Manly and overlooked Bongin Bongin Beach, at today's Grandview Parade. After the population diminished, the church was moved in 1888 by a bullock team to near George McIntosh's selection, Winnererremy, on Bay View Road. By 1907 a new stone church was built on its present site on Pittwater Road. In 1955 a front porch was added to the building and in 1982 the church was extended. The *Sydney Morning Herald* of 2 October 1897 declared St John the Baptist to be the 'First church built in this part of the Colony'. Early pioneers were buried beside the original church, including William Sparks and George Cobb, who were killed while building Barrenjoey Lighthouse. The old headstones remain.

Dungarvon was built on land two doors down from the church. Judy Childs in a *Manly Warringah Journal* states the land was owned by Samuel Stringer, a carpenter of Pittwater and was part of six blocks he purchased from the Mona Vale Estate. A local stonemason, James Booth may have done the stonework of the house and Stringer, the carpentry. Built c1904, the ashlar sandstone may have come from Brock's Folly. The symmetrical house, with its rooftop tower, attracts attention. Stringer resided at Dungarvon until 1922 and later residents included Harold and Mabel Squire. Harold Squire was the sculptor of 'Peter on the bullock cart' and filled his garden with sculptures. From 1957 the old house deteriorated until 1978, when it was sold and gradually restored.

Mona Vale Headland has grassy areas and a scenic lookout point. This 1980s view shows Pittwater, with craft of the Royal Motor Yacht Club and the Royal Prince Alfred Yacht Club to the right, and the western foreshores beyond. (Warringah Library Local Studies)

The Rock Lily Hotel

The Rock Lily Hotel has witnessed the traffic of Pittwater Road at Mona Vale since 1886. Part of the grant to Thomas Collins, it passed on to Frenchman, Leon Houreux, a former Warriewood timber getter, rumoured to have operated an illicit still in the scrub. The bricks for the low roofed hotel were hauled from Austin's Brickworks at Bayview and the hotel opened for business in 1887, named for the local rock lilies, or rock orchids, then prevalent in the area.

Passing coaches, private vehicles and scattered locals soon stopped for refreshments at the Rock Lily. The menu was said to be extensive and such amusements as quoits, skittles and swings were provided for patrons. They could relax under a grapevine-covered arbour at the rear of the building. Their host was a burly man of 20 stone who operated his own coach line from Manly from 1894. He dressed in white breeches and knee high boots and urged his five horses along with a whip. His mistress, the earthy Madame Boutin, managed the business for 20 years, before departing for the Narrabeen Hotel. Houreux decorated the hotel with his murals and risqué paintings. On his death in 1907 his married daughter and her husband, Madame and Monsieur Briquet took charge. By 1913 the Rock Lily was unlicensed but the Briquets lived on in the rambling building, while local children feasted on their flourishing grapes. A portion of the building became a butcher's shop. Houreux had built St Helena which overlooked the sandhills and Mona Vale Beach and his daughter and her husband later leased it to visitors.

There was a revival of the Rock Lily in 1947 and some ten years later it became quite fashionable for wedding receptions and functions. The Rock Lily has had its ups and downs and has managed to survive, but never with the same character and colour as when Madame Bouton ran it with Gallic hospitality for 'city bon vivants'.

The last publican of the Rock Lily Hotel, Ernest Hope-Carter stands proudly outside his establishment c1907. (Warringah Library Local Studies)

Bungan Head

The name 'Bongin Bongin' was first recorded in a survey of 1814 and was part of Robert Campbell's 700 acre grant. Bushrangers Hill on Bungan Head is the highest point behind Bungan Beach, Mona Vale. On the foreshores is a rock pool and Bungan Head Reserve faces the Tasman Sea.

There were few families resident prior to the 1920s but a strange building appeared in 1919 when Gustaf Adolph Wilheim Albers commenced Bungan Castle. Albers arrived in Sydney from his native Germany while in his teens and studied art with Julian Ashton. Initially apprenticed to an art dealer and framer, N L Schmidt, Albers became manager of the firm before setting up in business himself. He had flair as an agent and represented some 60 artists, including Sydney Long, Sir Arthur Streeton and Sir John Longstaff. In the 1890s Alfred Yewen built the cottage Bungania at the northern end of the beach at Bungan Head. Albers bartered one of Long's paintings, 'The Westwind' for land and began his home. He engaged an architect, J W Tristram, but Albers sketched his ideas on the beach. His rough, but comfortable 'castle', built of local stone, was completed in a year at the cost of £1100. Albers was soon dubbed 'The Baron'. Initially the residence was a weekender and there were parties for friends and artists. In 1944 Albers took up permanent residency among his furniture, relics and curios; one was a mummified cat. Bungan Castle was open to the public on occasions. When Albers died in 1959 his widow Ruperta continued to reside in the home until 1969. It then reverted to his great nephews, John and Robert Webeck.

Yewen arrived in Australia when he was 30 years of age. He had known William Morris of the Arts and Crafts movement and playwright George Bernard Shaw. Yewen had Labor Party associations and his politics were definitely to the left. He worked as a journalist in

Bungan Head: in the centre of the photograph is Albers's Bungan Castle, with Bungan Beach beyond.
(Warringah Library Local Studies)

Brisbane before joining the *Sydney Morning Herald* and compiling *Dalgety's Review*. When building Bungania, Yewen cycled to Bungan from Mosman. He married Margaret Alice Scott who was secretary at one time to Sir Henry Parkes, and artists, writers and philosophers were frequent visitors to their home.

Bungan Castle under construction, 1919; its owner, Adolph Albers, loved the area described by Ruth Park with 'its remarkable view, the richly-coloured cliffs and slopes garlanded with morning glory and bougainvillea, the ramshackle old weekend houses with semi-perpendicular winding lanes leading to them.' (Warringah Library Local Studies)

Brock's Folly, Mona Vale

George Brock was born in Balmain and later served as an alderman on Newtown Council. In the 1890s he inherited money and purchased land at Mona Vale, between today's Darley and Bassett Streets. He had a dream to establish The Oaks Polo Pony Stud Farm, together with a resort, The Hydro. He constructed a three storey, 37 room ornate building, which included dining areas, ball and billiard rooms, a ladies' lounge, smoking room, 25 bedrooms, bathrooms, kitchens and servants' quarters. The resort had its own sewerage system and water supply, a lake, fountains and statues, together with a polo field and stables. A number of small villas were also built. Brock believed an extended tramway service to Newport would bring visitors. Meanwhile he drove his clients from Manly Wharf in his own coach, it was claimed sometimes dangerously.

Unfortunately the tramway never materialised and Brock faced financial ruin. The estate, with 172 home sites, was sold to Arthur Rickard, Estate Agents, who unsuccessfully offered it for auction in 1907. The property became known as Brock's Folly. Restaurateur Rainaud, of Paris House in Phillip Street, then took over operation of the building as an elegant restaurant and guest house named La Corniche. In 1911 Arthur Rickard again unsuccessfully offered the property for auction. In the early hours of 8 January 1912 fire destroyed the main building, which the *Sydney Morning Herald* reported lit… 'up the country for miles around'.

M. Briquet of the Rock Lily, together with Henri de Possel, a Sydney shipping manager, rebuilt the burnt out La Corniche. W E N Abbott, a journalist and editor of the *Scone Advocate* holidayed as a child in the area. His memories were published in 1993. He recalled Monsieur Briquet's 'keen Gallic eyes' in his smallpox-marked face and how he roamed the beaches and rocks to fish, devising strange inventions. One was a revolutionary boat, named *The Wowser*, because it ran on water!

When completed, La Corniche was leased back to the Rainauds. Abbott recalled the neglected garden with a waterless fountain, depicting Apollo in a shelllike chariot, 'driving a team of spirited horses'.

During World War I La Corniche was a Red Cross centre for wounded soldiers. Later ventures as guest house, tea rooms and restaurant failed. In 1937 Questhaven Schools Pty Ltd leased the building as a progressive school. They moved to Melbourne prior to World War II. The Australian Air League held weekend camps and officer training schools until the property was sold to T Elliot, an estate agent, together with a partner in 1945. Elliot also had dreams for the site. It became the Pacific Country Club and later the restaurant El Matador opened briefly. The site looked sad and neglected and La Corniche was finally demolished to build home units.

LEFT: Emerging as a minature Napoleon, Brock's son Oswald steps from his elaborate birthday cake c1890. (Warringah Library Local Studies)

OPPOSITE: Built in 1894 by George Brock, this mansion was known as Brock's Folly and later La Corniche, Mona Vale Hydro, The Oaks and Pacific Paradise. (Mitchell Library, State Library of NSW)

Mona Vale Golf Club and Mona Vale Hospital

Beside Pittwater Road but screened from the traffic is Mona Vale Golf Club. The clubhouse is located off Golf Avenue, above Mona Vale Beach. It is an attractive course created from a swamp and sand dunes. An earlier golf course in the area was close by at Brock's Folly, built as a lure for land buyers but in disuse during World War I. Around 1920 a 3-hole course was made and began to attract players. In 1925 permission was given for a 9 hole course near Kitchener Park. It was created by voluntary labour and a greenkeeper was appointed in 1925. A proper club formed in October 1927.

The first clubhouse was a tent, then the disused local ambulance station was moved to the course as a new clubhouse. Warringah Shire Council drained the swamp in the centre of the course in the 1930s. During World War II the beach was lined with barbed wire entanglements. The clubhouse became an officers' mess for the army camp.

Following the war's end in 1945, normal life slowly resumed and the course reopened in 1947 and in 1956 extended to 18 holes. There was an official opening in 1960 but in September the following year the clubhouse was destroyed by fire, unfortunately, the club records were also lost. An igloo hut served as a temporary clubhouse until a new building opened in November 1983. Mona Vale Golf Club is a popular public course with wonderful views. The main lounge of the clubhouse is named for Centenary British Open winner, Kel Nagle.

Mona Vale Golf Club shares the area with Mona Vale Hospital, the first major public hospital on the peninsula. The land was granted in 1831 to Elizabeth Jenkins. Elizabeth bequeathed the estate to the Salvation Army with an agreement that her family be paid an annuity until the last member died.

The State government eventually resumed the land to build the hospital. A 152-bed acute care hospital was constructed. The hospital officially opened in March 1964. Twelve years later it was extended to include community health services, and a range of clinical services and facilities. From 2004 there was public concern about proposed changes to the hospital and a 'Save Mona Vale Hospital' Committee formed. In 2006 the State government proposed a new hospital would be built at Frenchs Forest, but maintained that Mona Vale Hospital would remain open.

Mona Vale Hospital opened in 1964 and it was the first public hospital to be built on the peninsula. Apart from private hospitals, the only other public hospital at the time was Manly Hospital.
(Mitchell Library, State Library of NSW)

The Zoo Farm – Mona Vale

Well known in the 1950s as the manufacturer of 'Silent Knight' refrigerators and as president and later Honorary Director of Taronga Zoo Park Trust, Sir Edward Hallstrom farmed 40 acres of land at Mona Vale. Earlier farmers had left because of flooding but Hallstrom drained the land and proceeded to grow banana shoots, clover, corn, elephant grass, lucerne, sweet potatoes and carrots as produce for Taronga Zoo. The zoo's manure helped fertilise the farm. The Zoo Trust later purchased the property for its original cost. The fodder produced there was not always suitable for some animals and with the establishment of the Western Plains Zoo, crops were produced at Dubbo. In 1975 the Hallstrom farm was rezoned for residential and light industrial and recreational use. Located between Bassett and Darley Streets, close to Pittwater Road, the farm is remembered in the street names Taronga Place and Hallstrom Place, Mona Vale.

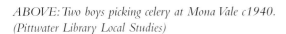

ABOVE: Two boys picking celery at Mona Vale c1940. (Pittwater Library Local Studies)

RIGHT: The army camp site of the 17th Battalion during World War II, looking towards Mona Vale Golf Course. Manoeuvres lasted two to three weeks. This area later became the site of Mona Vale Hospital. (Warringah Library Local Studies)

Terrey Hills Stores

Many will recall the general store at Terrey Hills, named for two early settlers Obadiah Terrey and Samuel Hills, who owned adjoining properties in the 1880s. In 1920 Hills grandson, Melbourne Samuel Hills, opened the Pioneer Store on Mona Vale Road, which closed in 1982 when Mona Vale Road was widened. The original Hills' land ran north almost to Tumbledown Dick. The name possibly dates back to the Oliver family. William Oliver, born in 1805, owned two lead bullocks, Henry and Richard, named for his father and father-in-law. The team hauled timber from McCarrs Creek to join the dirt Lane Cove Road (Mona Vale Road). Only two logs at a time were hauled up but on the last trip they pulled the last three up together. When they came to the steep part of the road the bullocks baulked and refused to go further. Dick was the left hand leader and the teamsters had to tumble the extra log off the load, and so the steep pinch became 'Tumble Down Dick'.

In 1935 five acres were purchased by Charles and Clara Grimshaw who emigrated from Britain in 1922. Charles and Clara slowly built their house, a shop and garage. They left in 1940 when the property was leased to Bertram Everest. In the war years USA forces were stationed at West Head and the shop flourished. Both stores are now just memories.

LEFT: The junction of Pittwater and Barrenjoey Roads, Mona Vale. To the left are the playing fields of Kitchener Park, no date. (Warringah Library Local Studies)

OPPOSITE: Newport developed on Pittwater and at the beach; this view is entitled 'Newport from the Quarry'. Early residences were often weekenders and Nancy Bluett (1984) recalled 'Our swimming costumes were made of woollen material, they were backless in the 20s or 30s. We always wore sandshoes and used to clean them with Bon Ami and pin them on the line to dry', from an oral history recording held at Mona Vale Library. (Roads and Traffic Authority)

NEWPORT

NEWPORT was a new port for coastal steamers to transport cargo and passengers between Pittwater and Sydney. The wharf was built in 1789 on the Pittwater side by George Pile and Charles Jeannerett. The Jeannerett family came to Sydney in 1829, worked in Tasmania and are associated with the history of Sydney's Hunters Hill. Early farms were owned by the Pittwater pioneers, John Farrell (1823), Martin Burke (1833), James Macdonald, Robert Melville, Richard Porter and Robert Henderson. When the wharf was built Farrell's grandson, Johnny, held 280 acres at Newport. Newport Beach was once Farrell's Beach. In 1888 Surveyor Bishop surveyed 'The Town of Newport'. On the Pittwater side 'Village Reserve' was set aside in this area perhaps as early as the 1830s.

In 1861 Newport Road to Barrenjoey Road was gazetted. When the wharf was built Jeannerett and Pile also built the Newport Hotel and subdivided the land for sale. They held the mail contract and this ensured all goods would be unloaded at their wharf. For a period Newport boomed as steamers called with cargo and passengers. Jeannerett encouraged visitors to travel by coach or steamer to visit the area and provided hospitality at the hotel. The 'Description of Newport, Pittwater and Hawkesbury Lakes' of 1881 commented favourably on the layout of Newport and declared 'A considerable trade has already sprung up, and as it is even now the centre of a very considerable population, the terminal point of an extensive system of river traffic, a favourite fishing locality, and a favourite place for yachting, and being more-over close to the ocean beach, Newport cannot fail to become very shortly a favourite watering place, and a town of considerable importance.'

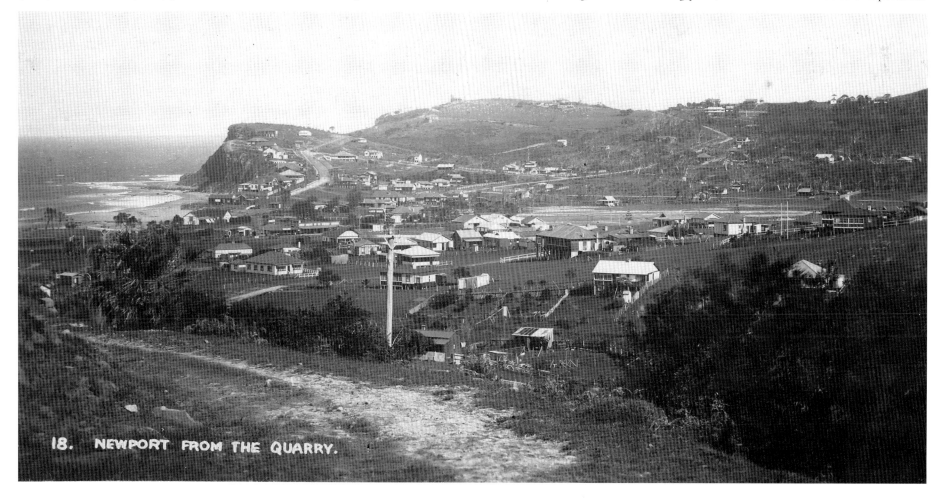

18. NEWPORT FROM THE QUARRY.

ABOVE: Three 'bathing belles' enjoying the ozone at Newport Rock Baths, 1928. (Warringah Library Local Studies)

LEFT: The Farrells were pioneers of Pittwater. Life was hard but Farrell's cottage at Newport offered hospitality and 'Hot Water' in the 1930s. (Manly, Warringah & Pittwater Historical Society)

A telegraph office opened at Newport in 1888 but it was another ten years before the post office was established. In 1905 Scott's Green Point estate was subdivided and sold through Arthur Rickard & Co. A lot of 66 feet could be purchased for £20, ten shillings down and five shillings a month. At the time Newport's population was only about 100 people and even with improved transport Newport remained a location for holiday makers. In 1906 two motor buses ran a trial service from Manly but the steepness of Sheep Station Hill rather defeated them. In 1918 the Newport Telephone Exchange boasted seven subscribers and the next year numbers climbed to ten.

Newport remained rural for many years with families keeping a few animals and producing their own vegetables. Meat came via the weekly steamer and local dairies, such as the Boultons, provided dairy products. The Farrells had a long association with Newport and at their barn provided a 'billy' of milk and allowed some to learn how to milk a cow.

The bails had a cobbled floor and were a slab construction. In 1928 there were 20 houses, a hotel, public school, a large motor garage and two shops at Newport. Within half a mile of the post office were 70 houses and within half a mile of the beach were three shops, an estate agent, a butcher's shop, 150 houses, a refreshment room and cabaret. About 40 per cent of the houses were holiday homes. From 1927 to 1931 the population increased from 133 to 175.

Holidays and weekends brought an influx of visitors and local stores, the Ocean Beach Store, Robertsons and Jurds the butchers provided necessities. In the 1920s, the area where Newport bowling green is located now, was Farrell's Lagoon, with many eels and quail about. A bridge crossed the water leading to the beach. The lagoon and marshland was filled in and an open concrete storm water channel was built under the Unemployment Relief Scheme of the Depression. People enjoyed simple pleasures with picnics to Bilgola Beach, dances to a gramophone, cards or a musical evening. At the beach was the Tea Pot Inn, built by the Middletons, who came from Mosman each weekend in

a horse driven sulky – until white ants devoured the building. New tearooms later included a small golf course. The world of kerosene lamps, horse rides to Palm Beach and rabbit shooting near Clareville ended with World War II but somehow even in the 1940s the local post office remained an annexe to Snape's General Store. During the 1950s Newport developed as a residential suburb.

First surf carnival at Newport January 1911. (Pittwater Library Local Studies)

A rather rickety Scott's Jetty in 1914. People arrived at the jetty by boat to stay at Scott's Boarding House. (Warringah Library Local Studies)

The southern end of Newport Beach and the opening of Farrell's Lagoon, crossed by the footbridge in the foreground, was photographed some time before 1918. (Pittwater Library Local Studies)

GREIG'S Newport Hotel, PITTWATER, via Manly.

The Only Licensed
Hotel in Newport.

Under Personal Management of
STUART GREIG for 14 years.

**Superior Accommodation
for Boarders.**

TERMS—From **6s.** per day,
or from **30s.** per week.
Children under 12 years Half Price.

TABLE D'HOTE, Daily and
Sundays, at 1 p.m., **2s.**

All Coaches Stop at
NEWPORT HOTEL. .

Boats and Motor Launches
Available. Baths Enclosed at
foot of Grounds. Dressing Shed
on Ocean Beach for Surfers.

Greig's Catering is noted
:: as Best in the District. ::

STUART GREIG, Proprietor.

View of Newport, with Hotel in foreground.

The Newport Hotel and Scott's – Newport

SITUATED by the waters of Pittwater, the hotel at Newport attracted passengers on the Sydney steamers. In 1887 the owners George Pile and Charles Jeannerett conveyed the hotel to William Boulton, who hailed from the Kalgoorlie goldfields. Within a short time he leased it to William Bulfin, although the hotel remained in the Boulton family until sold to Reschs Ltd in 1919.

Bulfin, an Irishman, arrived in Sydney in 1866 when he became a publican. Bulfin was also the Newport postmaster before his death in 1910. Charles Swancott recounts a story of when the hotel ran out of beer and supplies were brought from Manly. Unfortunately the axle of the cart broke on Bushrangers Hill and ten dozen of the 12 dozen bottles smashed. In 1938 broken bottles were still beside the roadside.

In 1891 Sir Henry Parkes opened an election campaign at the hotel, taking the opportunity to push his Federation plan. He promised two wharves and a public school. He was then Premier of NSW and the member for St Leonards.

There were wild times in 1892 when rival gangs of Pushes (gangs of unruly youths who operated in separate Sydney areas in the late nineteenth and early twentieth centuries) invaded the peace of Newport coming on the Sunday steamers. Drunken brawls broke out, often fuelled by illegal local grog, until the hotel manager, Tom Hodges, took the law into his own hands. On 14 February he recruited a couple of local boxers to greet the unruly visitors. Fruit was pelted, glasses

ABOVE: Stuart Greig's advertisement for the Newport Hotel shows the original weatherboard building of 1880. (Mitchell Library, State Library of NSW)

LEFT: Bayview House became Scott's Boarding House when Minnie Scott operated it from 1901 to 1914. It offered 'First Class Accommodation. Table d'hote 1 p.m. Afternoon Teas. All coaches start here.' (Manly, Warringah & Pittwater Historical Society)

The Newport Hotel and dusty road in 1905, appearing somewhat like a film set. (Warringah Library Local Studies)

smashed and an attempt made to wreck the hotel. The 'Battle of Newport' raged for a couple of hours until the steamer carried the Pushes back to Sydney. They wanted vengeance but after a rough passage the following week they had little fight left and peace returned to Newport.

The original small hotel, which stood in a picturesque spot at the head of a creek, was replaced with a brick building in 1919, following the auction by Richardson & Wrench Ltd, with more alterations made in the 1950s. Severely damaged in a fire in 1967, the hotel was rebuilt in 1971. The Newport Arms Hotel, which has had recent renovations totalling $2.5 million, is ideally situated with expansive views of Pittwater. It is a 40 minute drive from the Sydney CBD. During Heritage Week each year the hotel displays historic photographs.

There was a rival establishment to the Newport Hotel. Located not far away was Collins' Retreat and later Bayview House. In 1880 this building was leased to John Thomas Collins, who was married to Sarah Ann Farrell. It was originally the establishment of Daniel Farrell, and served refreshments to excursionists on the steamer *Kembla*, costing five shillings for adults, two and sixpence for children. In 1881 Sarah Collins, holder of a colonial wine licence, was charged with 'unlawfully selling spirituous liquor without a licence.' Sarah was accused of dabbling with brandy, schnapps and sly grog, although the charge was dismissed. In 1883 Sarah was

ABOVE: The rustic Newport Hotel in 1906 when it was operated by Stuart Greig, then later Elizabeth Grace Greig. Sarah Boulton leased it in 1914.
(Warringah Library Local Studies)

*LEFT: Film maker Arthur Shirley promoted his Ellerslie Studio productions with banners on the Diggers' buses. His company of stars are pictured here outside the 'new' Newport Hotel in the early 1920s. (*The Australian Screen*)*

489. PITTWATER N.S.W. FROM BAYVIEW HOUSE (H KING PHOTO SYD.)

NEWPORT NSW

charged again for the same offence. On appeal the conviction was upheld.

Boats were always available at the wharf for fishing parties and the steamer *Florrie* took tourists to Gosford and the Hawkesbury to enjoy 'Grand Mountain Scenery'. In 1886, for £100, Collins surrendered his unregistered lease of Bayview House and its six acres to the owner, Daniel Farrell. Farrell disposed of various holdings to Benjamin James, who in turn sold 25 acres to David Scott in 1887. Originally mortgaged, Scott owned the property by 1896. Bayview House became Scott's Boarding House, a respectable establishment with a high reputation for good food and comfortable accommodation. David Scott's daughter, Minnie ran the

High tide and placid waters of Pittwater as seen from Bayview House, Newport, by noted Sydney photographer, Henry King, c1873–1900.
(Warringah Library Local Studies)

boarding house from 1901 and was remembered as 'a very good cook', famous for her fish meals. Her brother Leighton operated a boat shed on Crystal Bay. In 1928 Scott's advertised 'Al Fresco Meals in Beautiful Surroundings – Dainty Dinners – Fish and Oyster Luncheons – Afternoon Teas'. Supper dances were arranged, orders taken for hampers, launches and yachts provisioned. Scott's closed in the late 1920s. During the 1930s the Andrews family rented the lower floor but the building was then demolished.

OPPOSITE ABOVE: Lovering Place, Newport, was named for Horace Lovering, who owned and subdivided the land in the 1950s. This view looks north over Lovering Place in the 1950s.
(Mitchell Library, State Library of NSW)

OPPOSITE LEFT: Newport in 1957, the era of the Holden.
(Warringah Library Local Studies)

RIGHT: Aerial view of Narrabeen Lakes, bridge, the junction of Wakehurst Parkway and Pittwater Road and Wimbledon Avenue 1967. (Roads and Traffic Authority)

NORTH NARRABEEN

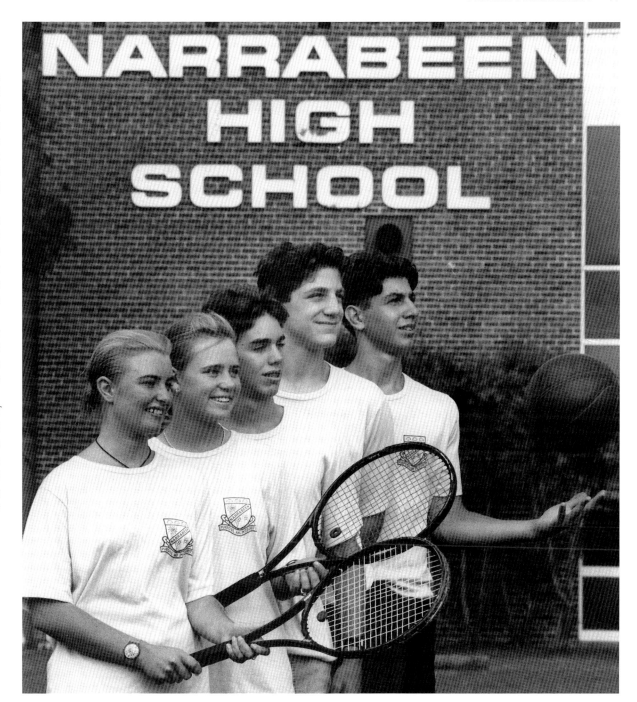

THERE are several versions of the origins of the name Narrabeen: from narrow beans consumed by Surgeon White of the First Fleet; a romantic tale of an Aboriginal girl, Narrabin, saving early settlers from convict murder; to surveyor James Meehan's Narrabang lagoon in 1814 (although in 1805 botanist George Caley named it Cabbage Tree Lagoon). In 1830 William Govett's survey marked Narrabine Lagoon and Narrabine Head.

Along the south bank of Mullet Creek land grants were given to John Lees (40 acres), Philip Schaffer (50 acres) and James Wheeler (80 acres). The Wheeler family had a long association with the Warringah and Pittwater areas. In 1815 Alex Macdonald held 80 acres at the beach and in the west 93.5 acres were owned by John Thomas Collins in 1857.

Small farms contended with floods and struggled for existence, apparently mainly growing corn and pumpkins. In the 1860s chubby, ragged children watched the coaches from Manly passing by on their way to the peninsula.

North Narrabeen is located on the coast, north of Narrabeen Lagoon, with Narrabeen Head and Turimetta Head as beach headlands. In the early 1900s the lagoon resembled a coastal river, with an ocean entrance further south, some 150 metres wide and 10 metres deep. This enabled small steamboats journeying between Sydney and Gosford to take on extra coal, near

OPPOSITE: Girls from Manly Girls High School attending a music camp at the National Fitness Centre North Narrabeen c1960.
(J Lanser, Pittwater Library Local Studies)

RIGHT: Five students outside Narrabeen Sports High School on 15 February 1994.
(Manly Daily)

the current location of the Pittwater Road bridge.

Narrabeen Head reserve has several lookouts. Bumper's Lookout remembers Frank 'Bumper' Farrell, a well-known 1940s and 1950s footballer and police officer who was Captain of Newtown Rugby League Club and at one time head of the Vice Squad. He owned land north of the lookout. Further north is Sheep Station Hill Lookout. In the 1880s coach passengers alighted to help push the coach to the top of the hill. There was no battle at Battleground picnic area but in the sea off the coast early vessels were wrecked on the rocks of Long Reef Point. Travellers in the nineteenth century had to cross the lakes in the coach by a ford, ladies raising their skirts and all lifting their feet to escape lapping water.

A bridge was built in 1880 and in 1925 a new bridge was commenced near the mouth of the lagoon in Ocean Street. The work was undertaken during a drought period and the lagoon dried up. At weekends enthusiasts watched speedcars and motor bikes with sidecars race on the lagoon bed. Bi-planes offered flights for ten shillings. At the time of the building of the new bridge and during five years of the late 1920s, the area at the mouth of the lagoon was dredged, which reunited the lagoon and the sea. The fill was used to reclaim swampland around the lagoon. Turimetta Head to the north has Sheoak, Cockle and Mullet Lookouts, reminders of what the Aborigines probably found in the area. There is also Boomerang Walk.

ABOVE: Widening of Sheep Station Hill between Narrabeen and Mona Vale in January 1957. (Roads and Traffic Authority)

LEFT: Pittwater Road, North Narrabeen, between Gondola Road and Namona Street c1962. (Roads and Traffic Authority)

OPPOSITE: A plaque commemorates the official opening of Wakehurst Parkway on 22 March 1946. (Pittwater Library Local Studies)

Mr Keilor and daughters in front of the truck the family lived in at Narrabeen Caravan Park during the Depression c1930s. (Ida Keilor, Pittwater Library Local Studies)

The extension of the tram to Narrabeen in 1913 brought holidaymakers and a popular camping area developed on the northern shore of the lagoon. In 1918 Pilson's confectionary shop opened in Octavia Street with hand churned ice cream. It became a butcher shop in 1925 when the area's few shops included a grocer, bakehouse and later a green grocer. Horse and carts made deliveries to residents, even delivering the mail.

Children roamed the local paddocks picking juicy blackberries, collecting mushrooms or swimming, fishing or prawning in the lagoon or lakes. There were boats to row up the lakes to explore the pristine creeks, and then enjoy a 'Gypsy tea' on the banks.

The hardships of the Depression put the unemployed on the dole, or 'sustenance'. A chant of the years was 'We're on the susso now, We can't afford a cow, We live in a tent, We pay no rent, We're on the susso now'. The homeless lived at camp sites at North Narrabeen and at Deep Creek. The Depression hit business at North Narrabeen. With 80 per cent of shop customers on the dole, local grocers were forced to close premises.

World War II saw local men enlist. The Wakehurst Parkway opened in 1946, providing road access from Frenchs Forest and Seaforth to North Narrabeen and Pittwater.

Pioneer of Flight

Despite a monument being erected at North Narrabeen, few remember an important event that occurred at Narrabeen in 1909. In the 1890s George Augustine Taylor (1872–1928) worked as a cartoonist on the *Bulletin* and *Punch* magazines. By 1900 Taylor became interested in town planning and helped found the Institute of Local Government Engineers of Australasia in 1909, and the Town Planning Association of New South Wales in 1913. An enthusiast of Lawrence Hargrave's experiments with flight, Taylor established a factory to make light aircraft, and worked on military uses of radio and telephones. Together with a group of enthusiasts, including Edward Hallstrom, Taylor constructed a manned glider. On 5 December 1909 Hallstrom and Taylor transported the glider to the North Narrabeen sandhills and initially flew it as a kite to ensure its stability and to test it would support a man. George Taylor took up a position beneath the lower wing and dipped and curved in a glide of 98 yards from three to 15 feet above the sand. He then travelled 258 yards and landed in the surf. Hallstrom also had a glide and then Taylor's wife Florence became airborne and the first woman to fly in Australia. Taylor made the first flight of a heavier-than-air machine in Australia.

Taylor promoted gliding in New South Wales and was a founder and secretary of the Australian Air League. He was also Australian administrator of the British Science Guild. A nephew, George Augustus Taylor (1902–1972) was an aeronaut and artist and his father was Vincent Patrick Taylor, known as Captain Penfold (1874–1930) a balloonist and stunt man who in 1914 dropped leaflets to promote the ferry to Clifton Gardens at Mosman. Flight was in their blood.

The Australian Aviation Museum, Bankstown, has a replica of Taylor's glider, manufactured by Mission Employment Punchbowl's Work for the Dole Team, under the supervision of Mr Brian Spring.

5. Collaroy looking towards Narrabeen, N.S.W.

George Taylor made the first flight of a heavier-than-air machine in Australia from the North Narrabeen sandhills on the 5 December 1909. He landed in the surf. (Warringah Library Local Studies)

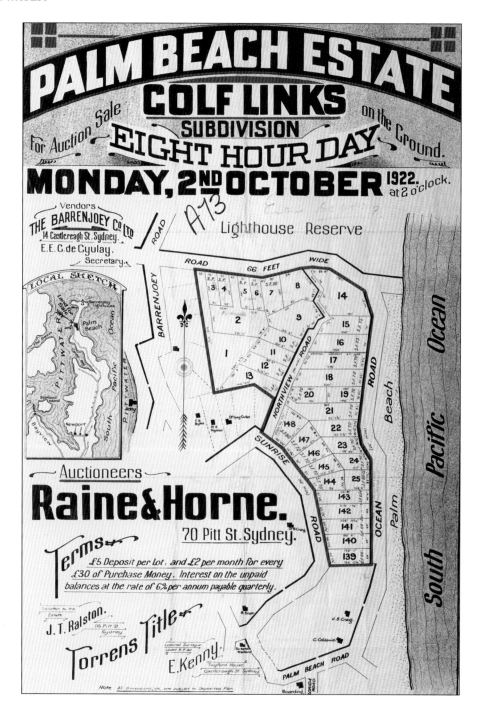

PALM BEACH

PERCEIVED as an escape for Sydney's social elite Palm Beach is named for its cabbage tree palms (*Livistona australis*). From 1832 the southern portion of the ocean beach has been Cabbage Tree Boat Harbour but at one time the beach was called Cranky Alice Beach. The area was part of James Napper's 1816 land grant of 400 acres, named Larkfield. Its isolation attracted fishermen, and it was undisturbed until the building of the Customs House (1843) and the lighthouse at Barrenjoey. In 1900 the Bassett-Darley Estate at Palm Beach was offered for auction, with 'marine sites' but the sale was a flop. More successful were two 1912 Raine & Horne sales of Barrenjoey Palm Beach Estate Pittwater, with a £2 lot deposit and the balance in monthly instalments of £1 per lot for every £30 of purchase money. Sunrise, Florida and Palm Beach Roads were named.

Transport was particularly difficult to Palm Beach. In *Setting out on the Voyage* (1998) author Nancy Phelan wrote 'When I first went to Palm Beach with my Aunt Amy [Amy Mack] there was no through road. We took trams to The Spit, to Manly, to Narrabeen, then a primitive bus over terrible roads to Newport harbour and a launch across Pittwater to Palm Beach, landing at Gow's Store, below Four Winds.'

LEFT: Palm Beach Estate Golf Links Subdivision, Sunrise Hill and Northview Road, 2 October 1922. (Pittwater Library Local Studies)

OPPOSITE: The view north-west from Sunrise Hill across Barrenjoey Beach to Lion Island and Barrenjoey Headland in 1912. (NSW Government Printing Office)

There were beach shacks, visitors surfed or walked to Barrenjoey Lighthouse or visited remote Pittwater beaches. With road improvements lorries carried people at weekends from Narrabeen. The Newport Road was completed c1920 and Barrenjoey Road was bitumenised at that time.

In 1912 Sunrise Cottage, built for surveyors, was rented by the Verrills family but later sold to James Robson-Scott. The Robson-Scotts commuted from Killara until they made the cottage their permanent home. Many of the houses were built by the Verrills family using local stone including a guesthouse, the first in the area, at the corner of Florida and Palm Beach Roads. In 1926 it was destroyed by fire.

Laurie Gallagher, a Scottish stonemason, built Florida House a licensed guesthouse in the early days of World War I. At the time Sunrise Hill was a frenzy of building and a number of unmarried women built cottages, giving the name 'Spin' or 'Spinsters' Hill' to the area. Macquarie Street doctors were attracted to an area that became 'Pill Hill'.

ABOVE: The Bell residence at Palm Beach was surrounded by bushland, c1918.
(Laurie Seaman)

LEFT: Enjoying the seascape at Palm Beach in the 1920s are Grandmother Bell, friend Doosie/Dowsie and Emmie, the housekeeper. Note the building on the right is the former Peters' residence purchased by Palm Beach Lifesaving Club in 1954. (Warringah Library Local Studies)

OPPOSITE: Palm Beach in the 'roaring 1920s' was an entirely different scene from Palm Beach in the 2000s. (Warringah Library Local Studies)

An unspoiled Snapperman Beach in 1899 with only a lone boat on the sand. (Warringah Library Local Studies)

Frank Hurley's view in the 1940s of Snapperman Beach, Sand Point, Sandy Beach and Careel Bay in the distance. James Francis 'Frank' Hurley (1885–1962) was a leading photographer of the first half of the twentieth century. His career began with a Sydney postcard company in 1905. (National Library of Australia)

The natural beauty of Palm Beach attracted many and a surf club formed. Sydney military and civilian tailor, W Chorley built a house around 1913, which later became the Cabbage Tree Club (for wealthy businessmen and professionals). The Pacific Club formed in 1937, strictly for women, and it still functions. Both clubs were part of Palm Beach Surf Life Saving Club. Numerous prominent Sydney people discovered Palm Beach, including the Curlewis family and in the mid 1920s the Horderns. R J Hordern, a keen gardener, planted the Norfolk pines at the beach front. He gave part of his estate to be Hordern Park.

At Pittwater jetty was Booth's Store, the first in Palm Beach. In 1923 Albert Verrills built Barrenjoey House for Mr Resch, as a guest house and restaurant. It had the district's first telephone. The Gonsalves family has a long association with Palm Beach and, with Gow, they hired out boats and owned two fishing trawlers. They operated a dairy from 1917 and were stonemasons, storekeepers and boat builders.

Many of the homes are of interest, including Willeroon, (1923) listed by the National Trust of Australia (NSW), now demolished. Palm Beach attracted writers and artists and by the 1930s was considered 'fashionable'. In the 1940s Lady Coles built a

LEFT: *Local resident, Chrissie Seaman, enjoying the pounding surf at Palm Beach in the 1920s, where Bohemia met wealth.*
(Laurie Seaman)

OPPOSITE: *Messing about with boats near the wharf at Pittwater, Palm Beach c1940. (Peter Verrills)*

house above the rock pool of Cabbage Tree Boat Harbour. Double decker buses began to wind their way to Palm Beach terminus.

In 1962 high above the beach Gerald H Robinson, a church warden of St David's created The Bible Garden, inspired by one he visited in Bangor, Wales. The garden of his home, Sea Song, had the typical poor thin topsoil of the region but he planted many species mentioned in the Bible. The view north is highly rated. In 2002 a Friends of the Bible Garden formed when Brian Robinson, a Trustee of the garden, wished to sell the property and establish a similar garden in Canberra. In 2006 the garden was handed over to the Pittwater Council by the trust, founded in 1972. This will guarantee its conservation.

Generations have enjoyed Palm Beach as an idyllic escape from the pressures of the city lifestyle.

ABOVE: New float plane landing at Palm Beach 10 August 1994. (Joe Murphy, Manly Daily)

LEFT: A quiet time at the Palladium Restaurant, Palm Beach. In 1925 The Palladium and the Ozone Café were operated by 'Pop' Webster.
(Murray Views, Warringah Library Local Studies)

A postcard view of Snapperman Beach and Barrenjoey House with a plane on the beach and boats for hire in the 1940s. (Pittwater Library Local Studies)

ABOVE: A true fisherman's tale: a fine haul of kingfish netted in 1950 at Palm Beach. (Mr Bill Robinson, Warringah Library Local Studies)

*TOP LEFT: A day at the beach in the 1920s. Note the clothing, and the cars parked along the roadside.
(Laurie Seaman)*

*BOTTOM LEFT: Models and cars of the 1940s on a camera shoot at Palm Beach, with photographer Johnson.
(Carl and Caressa Gonsalves)*

*OPPOSITE: Plenty of fish in The Peggy and wide smiles from local fishermen at Cabbage Tree Boat Harbour, Palm Beach, 1950.
(Mrs Robinson, Warringah Library Local Studies)*

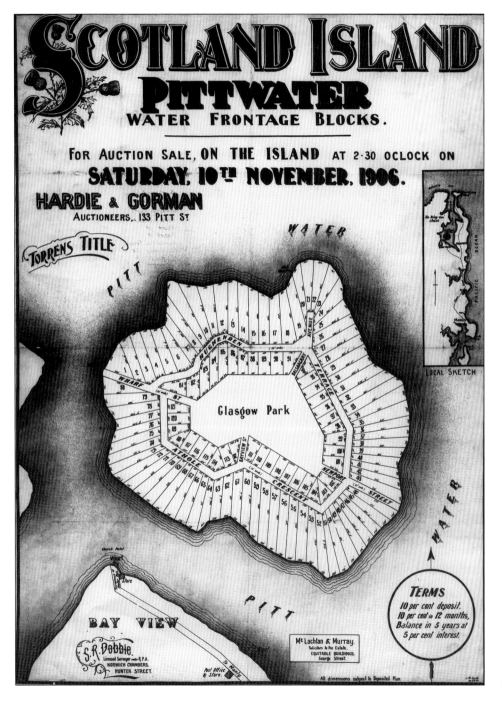

SCOTLAND ISLAND

SCOTLAND Island is a ferry ride from Church Point wharf. In March 1788 Governor Phillip named it Pitt Island. In 1809 Lieutenant Governor Paterson granted Andrew Thompson '120 acres on island near the southern extremity of Pittwater Bay…' with a rent of five shillings per year commencing after five years. In 1810 Thompson renamed the island Scotland Island after his homeland. Thompson was transported on the *Pitt* in 1792, sentenced to 14 years, for theft of cloth worth about £10. In 1793 he served with the police at Toongabbie and by 1797 he had an absolute pardon. In 1808 he was Chief Constable at Green Hills (Windsor). Governor Macquarie valued Thompson highly for 'he raised himself to a state of respectability and affluence'. On Mullet (Dangar) Island Thompson operated a salt manufacturing plant but moved the operation to Scotland Island. He extracted 200 lbs (90 kilograms) of salt a week from seawater by means of an oil burner. Thompson built a house and slipway on Scotland Island and was rumoured to have an illicit still. For three days and nights during the calamitous flooding of the Hawkesbury River at Windsor he worked to save lives and properties and endangered his own life. He died on 22 October 1810 at his Windsor home. Macquarie considered him 'the principal Founder' of Windsor.

Scotland Island was advertised in the *Sydney Gazette* in 1812 as 'containing 120 acres of good soil, extensive salt works, a good dwelling house and stores, labourers' rooms and every convenience suitable for a fishery or shipbuilding'. In 1815 it was again advertised for sale and divided into 13 lots. Around 1819 the island was owned by Robert Lathrop Murray, who departed for Hobart in 1823. The island then remained unoccupied. In 1833 John Dickson assumed ownership and appointed trustees (including his children). New trustees were later appointed and John Dickson died c1843 in

Subdivision Plan for Scotland Island auction on the 10 November 1906. (Mitchell Library, State Library of NSW)

An ordered orchard on Rocky Point, with Scotland Island rising behind, as seen by photographer Charles Kerry who worked as a commercial photographer from 1875 to 1913.
(Warringah Library Local Studies)

London. In 1855 mariners, Joseph Bens and Charles Jenkins each leased a portion of the island and farmed and ran cattle. They paid rent to Dickson's agent until in 1859 they discovered he held no title. They constructed a pathway around the island and in 1892 both men were issued with Certificates of Title, but Jenkins died.

Joseph Bens/Binns, was from Antwerp, Belgium. He was in fact Ambrol Josef Diercknecht. He owned a number of vessels including the *William and Betsy* and the *Lady of the Lake*. His wife, Kathleen was described as a small, dark woman with gentle manners but able to row herself across to Scotland Island even in a stiff nor'wester. Her eccentricity in her later years led to tales of buried treasure on the island and Andrew Thompson's occupancy also caused tales of buried 'holey' dollars. There are also tales of an infamous Sydney 'madam' who secreted her wealth on the island. Bens died in 1900. In 1906 Scotland Island was divided into allotments, except for Glasgow (now Elizabeth) Park at the summit, and offered for auction by, Hardie & Gorman.

Scotland Island rises 120 metres above the sea at its highest point and the foreshore circumference is three kilometres. There are about 1000 residents, with most houses being permanent dwellings. In 1965 electricity was connected to the island. Water shortages can be a problem, and there is the danger of bush fires, but there is a rural fire brigade. The Water Police assist in island emergencies, a ferry carries residents to work, shopping, and children to school, although parking has presented problems at Church Point. In the 1980s and 1990s residents built the community hall and children's centre. Residents declare on the Scotland Island website that it 'comes with a love of our surroundings and our special feeling of isolation.'

ABOVE: The community pitches in to build a hall and children's centre on Scotland Island in 1980. (Dieter Engler, Pittwater Library Local Studies)

LEFT: Unknown to many Sydneysiders Scotland Island residents are both permanents and weekenders. Many of the houses hug the foreshores. (Warringah Library Local Studies)

WARRIEWOOD

THE Warriewood Valley was swampy land with two creeks, Narrabeen and Mullet, flowing through the area. James Jenkins Senior, a former convict, and his wife Elizabeth, were pioneers in the Warringah area with the family farm Long Reef recorded in early records. In 1829 James Jenkins was granted 350 acres in the Warriewood area, which he named Cabbage Tree Hill Farm. Jenkins died in 1835.

By 1886 the area was still scrub land and in 1886 Leon Houreux, later of the Rock Lily Hotel, was a timber getter and reputedly had an illicit still on a Narrabeen creek. Wakehurst Parkway at Narrabeen Lakes still evokes memories of the tangled bush and swamp lands of the nineteenth century, when stands of forest oak, grey gum, ironbark, mahogany, stringybark and turpentine still existed. Macpherson Road, which today joins Powderworks Road, is named for the Macpherson family's farm.

In 1906 the land was subdivided for farm and residential blocks. In 1906 Henry Halloran & Co, offered 'The Great Warriewood Estate'. Their publicity praised the high quality soil, declaring an adjoining estate sold produce within seven months and that 'Mr Duffy, with no labour but his own, obtained 43 pounds of peas from an area… '. The climate was salubrious, the temperature mild, plants and flowers flourished and all the farm blocks were 'in a sheltered vale, intersected by

ABOVE: Auctioneers, Henry F Halloran & Co, produced a booklet 'The Great Warriewood Estate' to promote sales of the property. (Warringah Library Local Studies)

RIGHT: Henry F Halloran & Co's plan for the auction of 'The Great Warriewood Estate', comprising nearly 500 acres offered township lots, hill sites and farm blocks. Also marked are the Rock Lily Hotel, Mr C P Harington's residence and farm, and Mr P Bourke's residence in 1906. (Warringah Library Local Studies)

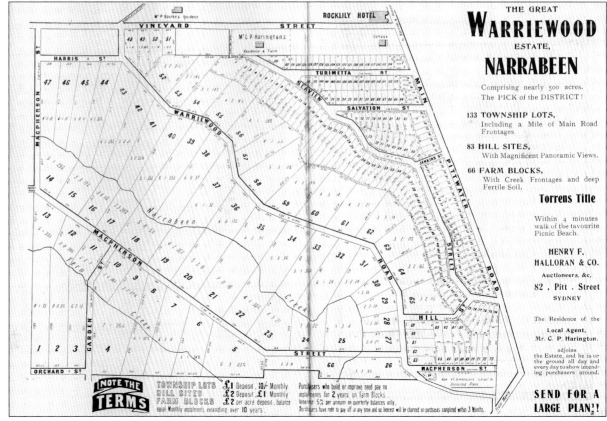

the Narrabeen and Fern Creeks' and protected from winds by a ridge and a range of rocky hills. There was no frost and three crops of potatoes could be obtained in a year from the one piece of land. They were eloquent about the excellent loamy soil and fine coastal rainfall. The farm lots sold well but the residential lots were somewhat premature to attract clientele. In 1911 with expectations of a tram service to Pittwater the sites sold well.

By the 1930s glasshouses mushroomed on the farm lots. Yugoslavia was a source of immigrants, who came to Australia seeking opportunity, because of poverty in their homeland. In 1933 the census revealed about 1000 Yugoslav immigrants in Australia. In the early 1930s there were some glasshouses at Warriewood, producing tomatoes. Serbians and Croatians were attracted to the industry and all worked hard in family units seven days a week. Eventually some 3500 glasshouses spilled over Warriewood and parts of Mona Vale, field crops were grown too.

The boom period of production was between 1947 and 1954 but by the 1960s the market declined and 'Glass City', as the area was sometimes referred to, dwindled to a few surviving glasshouses and plant nurseries. Light industry infiltrated, although the district was zoned as a rural area until 1991. The last garden nurseries disappeared with subdivision and Warriewood expanded with new homes and townhouses, the glasshouses a ghostly memory.

ABOVE: 'The Great Warriewood Estate' publicity booklet depicted the thick native vegetation to illustrate the richness of the soil. (Warringah Library Local Studies)

LEFT: An aerial view of Warriewood Valley showing the glasshouses and orchards in 1928.
(Edgar Longley, Pittwater Library Local Studies)

OPPOSITE: A double decker bus passing along Pittwater Road, Warriewood, in 1948 was good for sightseeing.
(Roads and Traffic Authority)

Warriewood Wetlands

Despite the changing face of Warriewood in recent years, the Warriewood Wetlands survive, the largest remaining sand plain wetland in the northern Sydney area. The area provides habitat for many migratory and local bird species making it a favourite spot for bird watchers. In addition it supports mammals, reptiles, amphibians, fish and insects. Because of a major shortage of public open space in Ingleside, Elanora Heights and Warriewood the Narrabeen Lagoon committee in 1978 proposed a Bicentennial Park. There was considerable public opposition to the wetlands being lost during the development of Warriewood Square Shopping Centre. Planned to protect an important catchment area for Narrabeen Lagoon, wildlife, migratory bird species and original flora, the park was to act as a buffer area for urbanisation and as a rich study area. The Warriewood Wetlands cover some 26 hectares and are the focal point of the park. The land was privately owned and Pittwater Council purchased it. Pittwater Council manages the Warriewood Valley, including the wetlands. The Warriewood Valley creeks, Narrabeen, Mullet and Fern also underwent major transformation with progressive restoration of creek line corridors. It is planned to plant between 10 000 and 12 000 trees in the valley in a five year period. A series of boardwalks facilitate public access. Local schools use the wetlands for educational purposes where they can see, hear, smell and feel the environment and enjoy the waterfall area. The Coastal Environment Centre, another Pittwater Council facility located on the northern shores of Narrabeen Lagoon, provides environmental information, educational and recreational activities for a broad audience.

LEFT: The head of Lovett Bay, Ku-ring-gai Chase, from 'The Great Warriewood Estate' booklet for Henry F Halloran & Co, Auctioneers, no date. (Warringah Library Local Studies)

THE WESTERN FORESHORES

PITTWATER'S Western Foreshores is a world of bays, beaches and wooded hillsides with a rich history of shipwrecks, early settlers and characters. Much of this history has been covered by local historians such as Dr James 'Jim' Macken, Audrey Shepherd, Sue Gould and many others who have a love and appreciation of this secluded world. As Sue Gould wrote in her book *Coasters Retreat:* '… the sheltered cove of Coasters Retreat and the placid sanctuary-like waters of The Basin form a haven, a retreat.'

This was the territory of the local saltwater people who walked their dreaming tracks, skimmed Pittwater in their frail vessels, fished, gathered and hunted. In 1998 Pittwater Council in a Statement of Reconciliation acknowledged their dispossession from their land.

A young woman secures a rowing boat with her bare feet. It is a cool day and a low tide in the 1920s. (Pittwater Library Local Studies)

Elvina Bay

Coming from the north at McCarrs Creek there is Elvina Bay, where the rugged terrain only allowed small areas to be farmed. By the mid 1860s the Olivers held 70 acres and in 1889 Arthur Wood had 40 acres. In this area they established orchards and kept grazing cows. Orchards produced not only citrus, but also figs, olives and flourishing vines. Surveyor Govett in 1829 noted 'the finest timber' in the recesses of the towering hillsides and the forest of red or forest oak was an extra source of money for William Oliver. Rocky Point, once named Flood's Peninsula for an early settler, was the site of Oliver's farm and later Trincomalee, home of the Neilsen family. The Ventnor Estate was subdivided in 1891 and bricks were made here by the Crawford Brothers, who resided in Ventnor. Early residents made use of nearby Linda Falls for their water supply.

Bushwalkers descending from West Head Road to Elvina Bay discover different vegetation on the shores from that on top of the ridges, where casuarina, cabbage tree palms and the burrawangs still grow. The ferry is accessible from Elvina Bay North, and Elvina Bay wharves. It passes Beashels Yacht Basin Pty Ltd, owned by one of Pittwater's yachting families. Colin Beashel was flag bearer for the Australian Olympic team at the 2004 Athens Olympics.

ABOVE: The old timber Palm Beach Wharf at Pittwater with waiting ferries, c1920s.
(Carl and Caressa Gonsalves)

RIGHT: A happy group of 1920s weekenders and holiday makers on a Pittwater ferry. (Carl and Caressa Gonsalves)

OPPOSITE: Looking across to the Royal Motor Yacht Club, during the Pittwater Regatta on 26th December 1936. (Mitchell Library, State Library of NSW)

Tranquility at Lovett Bay: writer Di Morrissey has recorded memories of her childhood at Lovett Bay where Dorothea Mackellar, actor Chips Rafferty, writer George Farwell and composer George English also lived. She recalled 'There was no power and it wasn't missed. The hiss from the Tilly lamp was comforting while you read and the kerosene lanterns were warm and friendly … '. (Mitchell Library, State Library of NSW)

The Chave sisters dressed in their tennis clothes. Their brother was Albert George Chave. In the 1880s the Chave family had the finest orchard in the district at Lovett Bay. Samuel Morrison, the first teacher of the little Methodist Church school at Church Point, married into the Chave family.
(Warringah Library Local Studies))

Lovett Bay

Captain Sidney R N surveyed Pittwater in 1868 and in 1869 named this inlet Night Bay. The spot attracted picnickers and walkers after the Ku-ring-gai Chase National Park opened in 1894, who climbed to Birnie Lookout (152 metres) above the bay. John Lovett settled here in 1836, his name appearing on an 1862 plan. In 1862 Andrew McCullock purchased 50 acres for £50 on the north of the bay, including the area of Hall's Wharf.

For bushwalkers the vegetation constantly changes with spotted gums giving way to xanthorrhoeas or grass trees, and angophoras. The understorey is diverse, including ti tree, hakea and grevilleas.

In 1924 Tarrangaua, the home of Dorothea Mackellar famous for her poem *My Country*, was built above Lovett Bay. It was designed by William Hardy Wilson (1881–1955) architect and writer, famous for his drawings and his love of Georgian architecture. Pittwater has attracted writers, artists and actors past and present. Another Australian icon of film, 'Chips' Rafferty, and his wife, were once residents of this bushland retreat. Gordon Andrews (1914–2001), a noted graphic and industrial designer lived at Wahroonga and Neutral Bay but later chose Lovett Bay for his home. Despite an international reputation, he became recognised in Australia when he designed the original distinctive decimal banknotes in 1966.

A youth hostel operates at Lovett Bay, accessible from Hall's Wharf. Originally a private residence, built in 1915, the building is heritage listed for architectural merit. A keen bushwalker and conservationist, Ibena Isles generously gave her home to the Youth Hostel organisation when she moved to the Blue Mountains. It is an ideal location with plenty of bush and water activities for young back-packers and others.

*Lovett Bay Boat Shed and wharf after bushfire damage in January 1994. (*Manly Daily*)*

Towlers Bay

Captain Sidney named this inlet Morning Bay, but it became known as Towlers Bay for Bill Towler, who camped here. Towering behind all the western foreshores is the bushland of Ku-ring-gai Chase National Park and high above Towlers Bay is the Bairne Trig Station. Towlers Track gives bushwalkers access to the bay from the national park. A portion of the foreshore was a depot for the Explosives Department, Department of Mines, with two cottages, boatshed, workshop and jetty. The main facility for explosives was at Bantry Bay but a powder hulk was moored in the bay at Towlers. The former Ku-ring-gai Chase Trust held three acres on the northern shore and they had one cottage for staff and another for public use. The early 1900s saw the jetty extended, and a bathing pool and a slipway for launches built in the bay. In 1911 a stone jetty replaced the original timber one. Adventurous souls made use of the tracks the Chase Trust constructed in 1909, 1912 and 1913 to Towlers Lookout, the Bairne Trig Station and The Basin.

LEFT: The rough jetty and walkway at Towlers Bay on the Western Foreshores with the Roma Guest House on the lower hillside in 1912. (Warringah Library Local Studies)

OPPOSITE: An aerial view of the Basin at Coasters Retreat on the day they put the net across the Basin, 27 February 1972. (Manly Daily)

The Basin and Coasters Retreat

From the bay heading north the names are Longnose, Pugnose and Portuguese Beach. Soldiers Point was granted in 1842 to John Andrews, a veteran British sergeant. The name Coasters Retreat is self-explanatory as small coastal vessels sought shelter here from southerly gales. Land was 'promised' here in the early 1820s, so early names associated with the area include John Clarke, whose land was conveyed to Martin Burke and the abovementioned John Andrews, who lived on his grant with his wife, Hannah until 1872. Life at Coasters Retreat looks idyllic, but even today residents may find life hard but 'it's worth it.' The south-western corner of Coasters Retreat was called Bonnie Doon Bay or Bonnie Doon Beach by the Trustees of Ku-ring-gai Chase. With shallow water, a sandy beach, a grassy flat and a stream across the beach, it was a popular spot for picnickers and visitors. A stone wharf, now heritage listed, and a 1914 retaining wall are distinctive features.

A portion of this area is The Basin, possibly named during Captain Hunter's 1789 survey. Jim Macken states the name was well-established prior to 1835. It is referred to in the grant that year to Robert McIntosh. Early settlers built terraces on the northern hillside to the west to grow their vegetables.

Both areas evoke strong passions in residents. Some have written histories of these communities. Their work is a compilation of the people, stories and memories from early times. Tales of earlier days include Ku-ring-gai Chase employees, local families, 1920s holidays at Bonnie Doon campsite, the yachting fraternity, Depression hardships when workers did everything to keep their jobs and 'near enough wasn't good enough', seaweed gathered for garden crops, visitors and campers, the little steamer *Eringhai* bringing vegetables to the wharf, or a tale of a local cow eating the Christmas pudding and children poking cow pats with sticks for days hoping to recover their Christmas threepences; it all makes a rich tapestry.

Sally of The Basin

Anyone reading of the Western Foreshore soon encounters Sally Morris of The Basin. Her story dates back to colonial days and, as told by Jim Macken, is a remarkable tale. At Pittwater Sally became 'the yachties' friend'. She arrived in Sydney in 1837 as an infant with her father, the Reverend James Allan, her mother died during the voyage. Little Mary Ann was cared for by a farming family at Windsor named Morris and the child became Sally Morris. It appears she had not only lost her mother, but her father was sent to Braidwood and their connections ceased. Sally eventually married the eldest Morris son. At the end of the 1860s the entire Morris family moved and squatted at The Basin. Sally's husband died but she was kept busy helping the Morris family and caring for various children.

Life was primitive with no established school and the worry of illness but there was much to enjoy in this environment. Sally became guardian of one of the Morris children, James, and cared for the children of

ABOVE: Sally 'Peggy' Morris's cottage at The Basin. Her bath was a stone formation in the creek. Following her death in 1921 the cottage was used by the Ku-ring-gai Chase Trust. (Warringah Library Local Studies)

LEFT: Sally Morris outside her home at the Basin, also E Solomon, Mr Robson and Mr Hughes and his grandson, 1918. (G Solomon)

OPPOSITE: The Pittwater Regatta was held annually on the Anniversary (later Australia) Day weekend in January, starting in 1907. It attracted Sydney yachtsmen who stopped over at the Basin. This beautiful yacht is from the era remembered by Sydney yachtsman, Ray Hollingsworth, who recalled 'In those days yachts didn't have engines nor water pumps and we rowed ashore to collect water in our demijohns – narrow necked stoneware bottles covered with wickerwork.' (Mitchell Library, State Library of NSW)

The Oatley family Camping at the Basin 1911. (Oatley family album, Pittwater Library Local Studies)

The Lucinda Weekend

There is local pride in the role Pittwater played in Federation. In the 1890s there was discussion concerning Federation and a proposal to draft a constitution. Sir Samuel Griffith, president of a committee formed to make recommendations for a federal constitution, suggested a weekend of discussion on *Lucinda*, a steam paddle vessel owned by the Queensland government. On Good Friday in March 1891 the vessel sailed from Sydney to the Hawkesbury but during stormy conditions sheltered in Refuge Bay. On the Saturday they sailed around to The Basin, a popular rendezvous for the local yachtsmen. In his diary Sir Samuel recorded that on '28th Saturday: At work all day with Kingston and Barton, Downer… '. Kingston, Barton, Clark, Downer and Wise were leaders of the convention. Edmund Barton became our first prime minister in 1901. On Sunday the committee members and the *Lucinda* sailed out of Broken Bay. Jim Macken has worked to commemorate the event and a plaque was erected at The Basin by the Commonwealth Government for the Coasters Retreat Historical Society to record the visit, which includes the statement that the Easter 1891 visit 'led to breaking the deadlock over contentious issues which eventually led to the adoption of the Australian Constitution.' Lucinda Park in Nabilla Street, Palm Beach on the opposite shore of Pittwater commemorated the event in 2001.

later settlers. In 1881 when Frederick J Jackson purchased The Basin, the Morris family had no legal claim to the land. Jackson held 50 acres of the flat at The Basin when workmen arrived to erect his weekender, Beechwood. Fortunately and astutely, Jackson befriended Sally, making her caretaker of his property. Sally continued to live in her little wooden hut where she had a couple of lodgers. In photographs Sally appears as a nineteenth century figure with her long skirt, apron, high necked, long sleeved blouse and old hat. Ten years into the new century there was a dispute with Jackson over the land, settled when Jackson gave Sally a life-time lease. Sally witnessed local wrecks, befriended ships' crews, was visited by friends and

became an identity to the yachting fraternity, whom she warmed with hot tea or soup after a day's racing. The 'yachtie's' called her 'Peggy' Morris. Sally cared for five state wards; one, Jimmy, stayed until she died. She must have been bereft during World War I when her wards enlisted and yachting was abandoned. Sally lived at The Basin for 50 years and died there on 6 June 1921 at the age of 84 years. She was buried at Manly Cemetery. In 1922 local yachtsmen erected a memorial to Sally.

Sally's hut passed to the Trustees of Ku-ring-gai Chase and was used as a Trust Lodge. In recent times Jackson's Beechwood was restored and now has a heritage listing.

OPPOSITE TOP: The south and east aspects of Midholme at Currawong on the 12 February 1992.
(Milan Scepanovic, Manly Daily)

OPPOSITE BELOW: The north and west aspects of Midholme on the 4 December 1992.
(Mark Scott, Manly Daily)

Currawong and Great Mackerel Beach

On the shores beneath the heights of the Lambert Peninsula are Currawong and Great Mackerel Beach. Currawong had been called Little Mackerel Beach and 'Wilson's' after the family who lived there for some years. The name Mackerel derives from the plentiful amount of that species in the waters. Both areas were surveyed by J Larmer in 1832. Martin Burke held 40 acres at Little Mackerel and 60 at Great Mackerel Beach, with Kirby's farm located at the northern end of Great Mackerel Beach.

During the 1830s many vessels sought shelter, while a number were wrecked in gales in Broken Bay. In 1834 Burke sold 40 acres at Great Mackerel Beach to James Marks but claimed the right to occupy the farm. Ellen, a daughter of Flynn (of Palm Beach), was a favourite of Burke and he gave her a 40 acre farm at Little Mackerel, which her father farmed. It was sold in 1854 to Cornelius Sheehan. John Clarke, another landholder and old soldier, died sometime between 1837 and 1841 and was buried at Great Mackerel Beach. In 1841 there were three families on Little Mackerel and Great Mackerel Beaches. The houses were simple wooden huts, with gardens, orchards, outbuildings, stables and yards.

In the 1920s H W Horning offered Great Mackerel Beach, Ku-ring-gai Chase as 'the only REMAINING BEACH ON PITTWATER, and facing its GOLDEN SANDS are the splendid blocks included in this subdivision… a DELIGHTFUL CHANCE FOR THE CITY WORKER'. As Peter Spearritt points out in *Sydney Since the Twenties* few city workers owned cars and to reach Great Mackerel they would have journeyed via train or tram, motor bus and launch.

Honorah Collins of Coasters Retreat claimed Sarah Wilson and her husband held land from 1872. Land ownership was a complicated affair until 1885 when disputes between various settlers were settled by the courts. The area was desirable with rich soil and a good water supply from the valley creek. The Wilsons became the owners of Little Mackerel. Mrs Wilson sold her property to her son-in-law John Sanderson in 1908. A

Newtown doctor and his wife, Bernard and Pink Marie Stiles arrived at 'the only private beach in all of Pittwater' and in 1910 purchased Little Mackerel Beach for £600. It was a beautiful unspoiled area with supplies brought by Sydney steamers twice weekly before they sailed onto the Hawkesbury and Windsor, returning with produce for the Sydney markets.

Children from The Basin would walk along the bush track to Little Mackerel to catch Agar's ferry to school at Newport. Sally Morris had a jersey bull, considered dangerous, which wandered to Little Mackerel and had to be herded and returned to The Basin. When the mullet were running, a lookout climbed a high tree on a headland to watch the fish and alert the fishermen. They hauled in good catches and transported them by train from Brooklyn to the city markets. At that time wildflowers were prolific through the bushland. In 1927 the Wild Flowers and Native Plants Protection Act was passed and in December that year two men were arrested at Duffy's Forest for stealing Christmas bells. Koalas and wallabies were to be found in the bushland and walkers could be rewarded with the sighting of a lyre bird.

The Ku-ring-gai Chase Trust wanted the coastal beach areas preserved but the State Government failed to co-operate. The Stiles built Midholme on 52 acres and Bernard Stiles, the son, remembered his father was friendly with the local fishermen. He recalled Dr E Blackwell, who owned land at Little Mackerel Beach and offered blocks of land for sale one Australia Day. The auction on 26 January 1920 by H W Horning & Co Ltd described the beach as being of 'semi-circular white sand', with 'hard white sand' beneath the water. The auctioneers painted a picture of 'sylvan loveliness'. Stiles later sold this area to the Port Jackson and Manly Steam Ship Company, who operated the Manly ferries. In 1949 it was sold to the New South Wales Labor Council, with a number of cabins erected as holiday spots for union members. In December 1999 Pittwater Council recommended that Currawong (Little Mackerel Beach) be included on the Schedule of Heritage Conservation Areas in the current Pittwater

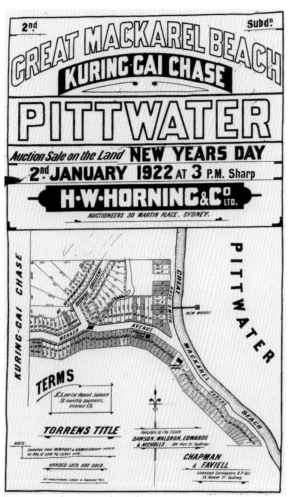

(Pittwater Library Local Studies)

LEP. Midholme, (1911) the Federation farmhouse, was listed on the State Register in 1993 and gazetted in February 1994. It was also listed on the National Trust Register because of its historical significance as one of the earliest surviving residential buildings on the Pittwater foreshores. In 1999 the National Trust of Australia (NSW) also recommended that the buildings, especially the intact group of early post-World War II prefabricated holiday cottages, be protected by a

conservation order. On 3 March 2001 the National Trust included Currawong on its register, recognising that Currawong has aesthetic, historical, architectural, archaeological and social significance to Australia. There is a 'Friends of Currawong' organisation.

A 1989 heritage study lists the former Shifting Sands at the northern end of Little Mackerel Beach as an archaeological site. The heritage officer was told by a visitor that it was built by a retired sea captain for a bride from the south seas islands who never arrived. The property was demolished in the 1970s.

Tribute should be paid to the men of the Pittwater ferries for they have always been the lifeblood of the Pittwater communities. In the 1960s and 1970s the McKay family operated services, the two ferries *Mirigini* and *Raluana* had a capacity of 180 passengers. In 1977 the service was sold to Peter Verrills, a familiar name in Pittwater. They have carried locals back and forth across Pittwater, taken children to school, and transported workers, shoppers and holidaymakers. The family sold the ferry service recently. There is romance to these little vessels, somehow reminiscent of the old ferries that once operated in the Scottish islands.

OPPOSITE: A 1950s view of Great Mackerel Beach. It shows the northern barrier-dune extension, a feature that trains the stream mouth against the far headland. (Warringah Library Local Studies)

Ku-ring-gai Chase National Park

Only 25 kilometres from Sydney Ku-ring-gai Chase National Park covers 14 882 hectares of sandstone bushland and is Australia's second oldest national park, after the Royal National Park. It is the oldest national park established primarily for nature conservation and is one of the top ranking biodiversity reserves. It is an area with great cultural and spiritual importance for indigenous Australians, with more than 800 Aboriginal sites such as rock engravings, hand stencils, grinding grooves, stone arrangements, burials and occupation sites.

The park is ranked in the top ten natural heritage hotspots identified for its importance for Gondwanan or primitive species. It has a wide variety of native flora, fauna and birdlife and offers a variety of walks, stunning scenic views and provides an escape from the city.

Within today's park an area of 640 acres (260 hectares) from West Head to Flint and Steel Point was granted to William Lawson, one of the party who crossed the Blue Mountains in 1813. Ku-ring-gai Chase National Park and associated reserves are listed on the Register of the National Estate.

This area was proclaimed a national park through the efforts of Eccleston du Faur. Born in England in 1832, du Faur migrated to Australia in 1853. After suffering hardship in the bush he returned to England but returned in 1863. He worked in the Surveyor General's Department and upon the death of his wife he commenced exploring the Blue Mountains. Perhaps this stimulated his love of the bush. In 1878 he remarried and settled at North Turramurra in Flowton (1895) now the administration block of the Lady Davidson Hospital.

For many years du Faur lobbied for 'a national park for North Sydney', even enticing the Governor the Earl of Jersey to view the proposed area. His park was established in 1894 with du Faur selecting the name. It was controlled by a Trust and du Faur was the first Managing Trustee. The park had no public subsidy until 1967 when control passed to the National Parks and Wildlife Service.

West Head was added to the national park in 1951 and is a popular vantage point with extensive views, including Pittwater, Barrenjoey Headland and Lion Island. In 1956 Lion Island was set aside as a fauna reserve. Ferries from Palm Beach operate to Bobbin Head and the park has various sites of historic value, including Beechwood cottage, several sandstone structures of importance, the Bobbin Jim, a sandstone war memorial near Turramurra, military observation posts and road access to a recreation area at Bobbin Head. The Visitors Centre is located at Kalkari (Bobbin Head).

Pittwater and Ku-ring-gai Chase National Park viewed by Charles Kerry, from Birnie Lookout, or Flagstaff Lookout. Lovett Bay is below, with the nearest promontory Rocky Point and Scotland Island centre left. Mona Vale is in the distance, c1890–1900. (National Library of Australia)

WHALE BEACH

FROM the heights of Whale Beach there are magnificent views of the Tasman Sea, but the origins of the name are unknown. Some claim it is from a whale washed ashore in the late nineteenth century, or after the whale shaped northern headland.

In 1816 it formed part of James Napper's land grant. Beautiful but lonely and isolated, the bush was thick with flannel flowers, Christmas bush and Christmas bells. When offered for sale in 1900 by the Barrenjoey Land Company the land did not sell, and the only inhabitants were weekend fishermen. In 1912 small blocks of land sold and the next year the Whale Beach kiosk was built to cater for the needs of weekend visitors. Water was carted from a standpipe at Mona Vale. Around 1918 Whale Beach Road was roughly built and in 1919 there was another real estate auction but Whale Beach remained undeveloped.

In 1927 the Palm Beach Land Company, which owned land from Palm Beach to Avalon, employed Jack Webster to build roads throughout the area. The company built Webster a house at Whale Beach, where food for him and other employees was brought on the steamer *Eringhai* to Palm Beach wharf and collected day or night depending on the tides. Their bread came via Greig's bus from a Narrabeen bakery but often the bread was flattened by passengers and was fed to the horses. Webster, busy building the roads, numbered the allotments of the Whale Beach subdivision. Gradually others arrived: the Mort, Du Boise, Lamb, Young and Geddes families. In November 1932 the vessel *Irvington* was wrecked at Whale Beach. For over 40 years Jack Webster lived in the family cottage at Whale Beach and witnessed the changes to the suburb.

Post World War II, with easier access and the increase in car ownership, Whale Beach developed as a desirable residential suburb. Jonah's on Bynya Road is a famous restaurant and now also a bed and breakfast facility. It began in 1929 as a roadhouse when an English woman, Constance Vidal, had the foresight to realise that the new fad for motor cars would make Whale Beach a desirable destination. Perched high above the ocean, diners may even sometimes glimpse a distant whale.

Whale Beach in 1945. It became a residential suburb post 1950s. 'Whale Beach was my first love on this peninsula and I confess it is still a special fancy. Once I never left its sun-drenched northern corner from the beginning of summer to its sad conclusion…' Phil Jarratt, 1988. (Warringah Library Local Studies)

An aerial study of Whale Beach and coastal headlands by noted photographer Frank Hurley. 'These Pittwater suburbs are amongst the most delectable districts in Sydney, almost tropical in style… Swimmers off the Peninsula beaches are often amazed by the coldness of summer waters; this is caused by the polar current, sweeping up through melting ice floes to cool the east coast of Australia', Ruth Park. (National Library of Australia)

SCHOOL DAYS

PITTWATER currently has an excellent range of public, private, Catholic and Montessori schools, with education commencing on the peninsula in the late nineteenth century. A small school opened in the tiny Church Point Chapel in 1884, called Pittwater Public School. It was replaced with a brick school and residence in 1888. In 1892 the name changed to Bayview School. In April 1888 the first school at Newport opened, called Mona Vale Provisional. By 1900 it grew to the rank of public school, and after Bayview School closed in 1906, numbers expanded. Mona Vale School opened in 1906 as a temporary school, to become permanent in 1911. Also in 1911 the present Pittwater Public School opened, built by James Booth, a local stonemason who had a quarry near today's Mona Vale Cemetery. More recent schools include Avalon Beach Public School, opened in 1950, Pittwater High School in 1963 and Barrenjoey High School in 1968.

On grandparents' days pupils enjoy hearing tales of 'What was it like when you were at school?' In the 1888–1900 period, punishments dealt with by the cane included cheating, indifference, fighting, truanting, disorder during scripture, stealing, deliberately pulling up each other's clothes in school, larrikinism, sullenness, throwing crusts and attending fire at lunch time! Despite the cane, some truanted and Pittwater children had a host of excuses – wanted at home, gone to Sydney, 'too far and too rough' from a child from Bayview, too lonely a route to school, free steamer to Bayview, dislike of teacher's methods, sickness at home, and one who was engaged at 13.6, presumably the pupil's age!

ABOVE: The Mobile Immunisation Clinic at Mona Vale Public School in 1953. Note the school bell.
(Warringah Library Local Studies)

RIGHT: Newport Public School, 1931.
(Warringah Library Local Studies)

Dressed in their 'Sunday best' the girls and boys of Mona Vale Public School assemble for the school photograph. The teachers, or parents, watch through the windows. (Herbert Wells, Warringah Library Local Studies)

WAR YEARS

THE years of World War II are remembered by the older generation of Pittwater. West Head, within Ku-ring-gai Chase National Park, has heritage listed fortifications and gun emplacements from the battery, completed in March 1941. Its task was to protect the Hawkesbury River Bridge and prevent enemy craft entering Pittwater and Cowan Creek. Similar to the boom in Sydney Harbour, there was an anti-submarine net between Barrenjoey and West Head, with an additional one positioned from Flat Rock Point to Little Wobby. From West Head to Lion Island, the navy installed a photo-electric beam to detect submarines or small craft at night. Around Sydney small boats were impounded and local Pittwater boat builders collected vessels in their area to anchor them in the Hawkesbury River well away from any invasion forces.

La Corniche at Mona Vale was used by the army, for an Infantry Training School for NCOs. Oral histories recall the impact on local lives when the army arrived and cut trees, dug ditches to make tank traps and built walls, about which one local declared '…the Japs were not going to be able to get up having come thousands of miles from Japan. We had barbed wire everywhere, to say nothing of the army, but the trouble was they didn't have any weapons. It was absolutely amazing. Bill and I went into hysterics except we were a bit worried what was going to happen. There were a couple of gun emplacements here… but nothing to put in them!' (Betty Morrison 1984).

The fear of invasion was very real, especially following the Japanese midget submarines attack on Sydney Harbour on 31 May 1942. Following that attack there were a number of reports of submarine sightings at Pittwater. Some Sydney beaches were protected with barbed wire barricades and concrete tetrahedrons to impede invaders. As Guy Jennings (*The Newport Story, 1788–1988*) notes there was a tank trap which stretched from Bungan Beach to Pittwater and passed close to the 11 Mile Store. A timber bridge spanned the tank trap

which was bolted together in such a way that if you knocked one bolt out, the whole bridge would fall into the trap. This bridge allowed cars to drive north along Barrenjoey Road, although there was little traffic with petrol rationing in force. It was mined with explosives for good measure. The trap was lined on the southern side with large poles which presented a high vertical barrier to any intruders. From the end of the tank trap there were large concrete blocks shaped like pyramids that extended part of the way up to Winji Jimmi. In the Avenue there was at least one fox hole and all the families living north of the tank trap had to be ready for evacuation at a moment's notice… As Newport had no barbed wire, servicemen came to swim and surf. Mr Vincent's house at the southern end of Myola Road was requisitioned by the army and fortified with a gun trained on the beach'.

It was a world of blackout curtains at night, air raid wardens, and bomb shelters built in suburban back yards, some stores and schools. At school, children had kit bags of bandages, sticking plaster, butterscotch and essentials and padded homemade helmets for protection during bombing. Older girls made camouflage nets and knitted socks, and everyone worked for the war effort.

At Ruskin Rowe there was the Sundown RAAF Camp, where the Women's Air Training Corps trained under the famous aviator, Nancy Bird Walton. They later moved to St Ives, where an important training area was established. The unit became part of the WAAAF, Women's Auxiliary Australian Air Force. Lookouts were posted between Warriewood and Barrenjoey. Refuge Bay on the Hawkesbury was selected as the site for a secret Camp X, a training base for 'Z' Force, Special Unit Commandos. The men were trained for a specific mission called *Jaywick*. The legend of the *Krait*, a former Japanese fishing boat, was born, its mission to attack enemy shipping in Singapore Harbour. Many recall the torpedo range operated by the RAN at Taylors Point from 1941 to 1983. Here torpedos were tested prior to being issued to submarines. Pontoons registered the speed and accuracy of the torpedos as they were fired. The wharf and firing station were dismantled in 1983 and, as part of *HMAS Penguin*, it became a diving and hydrographic school. The fear of invasion lessened after 1943 but at one time the site of Mona Vale Hospital was a tent city for trainee machine gunners.

At war's end there was a farewell march at St Ives to the Volunteer Defence Corps and a former barracks at West Head converted to a National Fitness Camp.

The tents of 'The Green Hornets' of the 7th Battalion Volunteer Defence Corps, at Warriewood Camp during World War II, 1940. (Warringah Library Local Studies)

YACHT CLUBS

YACHTING and sailing are a core element of Pittwater. With yacht charter firms, organisations such as Bayview Yacht Racing Association, Palm Beach Yacht Club and two major yachting clubs, this is not surprising. An Easter Camp was held at The Basin in 1900 and this occasion became a gathering of yacht people. The Basin Cup was sailed from Sydney Harbour to Broken Bay in 1906 and the following year the first Pittwater Regatta was held, then continued annually until 1979, with the exception of the years of World Wars I and II. It is not surprising Pittwater's yacht people have participated and won events in Olympic Games.

The Royal Prince Alfred Yacht Club formed in 1867. The members of the Mosquito Yacht Club met at McGrath's Hotel, Sydney, and adopted the name Prince Alfred as Queen Victoria's son, Prince Alfred, Duke of Edinburgh was to pay an official visit to Sydney in 1868. The Prince entered Sydney Harbour on *HMS Galatea* to be greeted by two lines of yachts from the Royal Sydney Yacht Squadron and The Royal Prince Alfred Yacht Club.

The Royal Prince Alfred Yacht Club, known to locals and members as The Alfred, has a long and colourful history. Initially the club met in Sydney and at one period had clubrooms at 9 Rowe Street, the fascinating little bohemian street, sadly demolished in 1974.

Enthusiasts gathered on a sunny January day in 1924 for Regatta Day at Pittwater. (Alan Sharpe)

Looking at Pittwater with the Royal Motor Yacht Club on the top left and the Royal Prince Alfred Yacht Club top centre. (Warringah Library Local Studies)

Eventually in 1919 land was purchased at Green Point, Pittwater. Lord Wakehurst, Governor of NSW, opened the club premises in a boatshed on 17 December 1938. During World War II the club closed from 1942 until 1946. The Royal Prince Alfred Montagu Island Race began in 1947 but was abandoned in 1987. Additional land was purchased and renovations made to the club. On 15 May 1968 another Duke of Edinburgh, Prince Philip, visited and set the stone for a new clubhouse during a strong nor'-westerly. In 1970 the club's headquarters transferred to Green Point from Rowe Street in the city. In 1967 a member of the club won the prestigious Admiral's Cup of the Royal Ocean Racing Club, Britain. In 2003 Bob Oatley of The Alfred won the Admiral's Cup with *Wild Oats*. In 1981 the club commenced the Pittwater to Coff's Harbour race, a challenging race of 226 nautical miles up the NSW coast. The club offers a wide range of sailing and social activities.

The Royal Motor Yacht Club Broken Bay has grown with the years from a small club of 'boaties' to a modern facility. It offers cruiser competition, sailing racing, sail cruising, power cruising, multihull sailing, game fishing, club watersports and twilight sailing. The original club opened in Rose Bay, Sydney in 1910 and the club formed at Pittwater in 1926 at Horse Shoe Cove. Access was via a dirt track before a new clubhouse rose in 1928, which was destroyed by fire in 1935. Another clubhouse was built but closed during World War II. Lady Cutler, wife of the NSW Governor opened a new clubhouse in 1968. The club has an extensive marina and has become an integral part of Newport and the yachting and boating life of Pittwater.

VJ dinghies racing off Clareville Beach c1930. (Isobel Bennett, Pittwater Library Local Studies)

SURF CLUBS

PITTWATER has always been a popular holiday area. Establishments such as Barrenjoey House (1923), a guesthouse and restaurant, catered for the holidaymakers. The post war period of the 1950s saw the development of more recreational facilities on the peninsula such as bowling, yachting and surfing clubs.

The Pittwater area is blessed with a string of beaches, which attract sun and sea lovers. There are surf clubs at North Narrabeen, Warriewood, Mona Vale, Bungan Beach, Newport, Avalon, Whale Beach, Palm Beach and North Palm Beach. The origins of the early clubs are a tribute to early life savers.

Several formed in the 1920s and Palm Beach, North Palm Beach and Avalon are examples of the growth of the surf life saving movement. Palm Beach Surf Life Saving Club formed in 1921, the first clubhouse was a wooden shed beside Powhokohat, the residence of the Peters family. Peters was involved in the construction of Burrenjuck Dam and the house was one of the first reinforced concrete private residences in Australia. Many club members lived in tents while attending the beach. The club badge was a cabbage tree palm on a circular backdrop in green and gold, selected by a veteran of World War I, J F 'John' Mant, from the colours of his First Battalion, First Australian Imperial Force. The first club surf reel was home made, with the surfboat, a three seat clinker built double-ender. The early boats were heavy and needed 12 men to carry them. The club relied on its female supporters to assist with fund raising activities.

Jean Retallack (Piper) posed on the North Palm Beach Surf Life Saving Club's first surf reel c1947.
(Warringah Library Local Studies)

The club moved to a second clubhouse at Hordern Park, close to the Hordern residence, not always a happy position. Their third was sited close to the original wooden shed. The fourth was Chorley's purchased in 1936. In 1913 W Chorley, a civilian and military tailor, built the two storey holiday cottage. Families, such as the Horderns were involved in the formation of the club and the Curlewis family later joined. Herbert Curlewis, his wife author, Ethel Turner and family first came to Freshwater in 1912 and gradually moved north. Their son, Judge Adrian Curlewis, born in 1921, became a noted surfer. He was president of the Surf Life Saving Association of Australia from 1933 to 1974, then sole Life Governor of that association from 1974, and President of the International Council of Surf Life Saving 1956 to 1973.

In 1936 dressing sheds were built on Palm Beach and the next year the Cabbage Tree Club formed. Palm Beach Surf Life Saving Club, Cabbage Tree and Pacific Club form one of the more exclusive clubs in New South Wales.

North Palm Beach SLSC, in Governor Phillip Park, had its origins in the Beacon Store in 1939. It closed during World War II, not to reform until 1946. It met initially in a tent until the old Avalon cricket club building was moved and erected at Barrenjoey. With added verandas it was used as clubhouse and Palm Beach kindergarten. A shark bell was located on the beach held aloft between two poles.

A foundation member in 1946 was Jean Retallack (Piper) and she often walked to the lighthouse and cared for the Mulhall grave. At the time women were only associate members and not full members until 1979.

Members of the Palm Beach Surf Life Saving Club show their flag at their second clubhouse at Hordern Park in the 1920s. Second from the left is Adrian Curlewis. (Carl and Caressa Gonsalves)

The associate members of the March Past Team of North Palm Beach Surf Life Saving Club c1948. The team, in sandals and white sharkskin costumes, is led by Jean Retallack (Piper). (Warringah Library Local Studies)

In 1971 fire destroyed much of club's equipment. When the old club was demolished, a new one opened on the site in 1973. The club initiated many patrolling methods and equipment as the club had the largest patrolled area in Sydney. The club used UHF radios to cover the distance, introduced a 'roving patrol' where members patrolled the beach away from the surf flags and they were the first surf club to own a four wheel drive to use as part of the beach patrol. The club attracts members from all over Sydney. They also hold a higher average of examiners, trainers and awards holders than many other surf clubs in Australia. Palm Beach is a location for the television series *Home and Away*.

Avalon Beach Surf Club was formed in 1925 by a group of young men at A J Small's house, Avalon. Small was the first patron. The next year an examination for the Bronze Medallion was held, with five successful candidates. While there was no clubhouse, Small provided the reel and flags were kept in the tennis court shed, with meetings in the general store. Apparently in 1929 there was no lifesaving service and an inspector complained an old wooden reel was well back from the beach with the line broken and tied in knots. The council offered a reel, line and belt as long as local residents were responsible for their being maintained. Meetings were held on the beach with drills of marching in the sand. In the mid 1920s equipment was one reel, one line and one belt valued at £10. It was in the early 1930s before another bronze squad was examined. In 1933 a club and new dressing sheds were proposed. Designed by local architect A S Jolly, they did not open until 1934. The clubhouse was dwarfed by the dressing sheds. During the Depression years some unemployed surf lifesavers from the city came and lived cheaply on the northern beaches. From such humble beginnings the club grew and early members would surely have appreciated the keenness of little Emma Howes, aged 8 years in 1995, who wanted to be a 'Nipper' at five years of age. Her memories are in *Sun, Sand and Surf*, published by Warringah Council. She loved Christmas when Santa came in a rubber ducky and threw out lollies, but she also recalled being caught in a rip when she found herself 'moving through the water really fast'. Good enough reason for the existence of surf life saving clubs.

LEFT: *The young men and women of Palm Beach Surf Board Club in the 1960s. (Carl and Caressa Gonsalves)*

OPPOSITE: *The Surf Life Saving Club Rooms, North Palm Beach, c1948.*
(Jean Piper, Warringah Library Local Studies)

Surf life savers at North Palm Beach in 1988. (Manly Daily)

BUSH FIRES

BUSH fires have been a part of Australian life since early settlement. Bush fires start slowly but the most dangerous fire is the one that roars and gusts through tree tops, creating a firestorm.

Between 27 December 1993 and 16 January 1994 the NSW eastern seaboard from the Queensland border to Bateman's Bay in the south and inland as far as Bathurst experienced 204 bushfires, destroying 800 000 hectares. The worst affected areas were the Hunter, Blue Mountains and Sydney regions, in particular the southern suburbs of Jannali and West Como. There were 136 separate fires in total in the Sydney region and the far North Coast. Residents of Pittwater and Warringah will not easily forget the fires that flamed through their areas that January. At that time there were 13 bush fire brigades in the Warringah/Pittwater area, responsible for 260 square kilometres of bushland and 4044 houses. Most of the early January fires were deliberately lit by arsonists. The origin of the Warringah/Pittwater conflagration was at Cottage Point at 4.28 in the afternoon on Friday 7 January, urged on by a strong north westerly. Virginia Macleod has written *Burnt Out? Experiences of the January 1994 Bush Fires in Warringah and Pittwater*, which gives dramatic accounts of the period when the skies turned red.

Residents of Bayview Heights watched horrified as 'a huge column of flame appeared on top of the ridge and West Head looked spectacular in a macabre sort of way, as the fire rushed towards McCarrs Creek Reserve.' Constant wind changes sent the fire in different directions. On the Saturday the Church Point bush ignited with the fire fighters needed in different areas, while a helicopter water-bombed. Residents recalled the cyclonic wind, a huge wall of fire and fires exploding around and above them. The following day the fire expanded enormously to McCarr's Creek,

Aftermath of the bushfires at West Head in January 1994. (Pittwater Library Local Studies)

Lovett and Elvina Bays and Bayview. At the same time another front erupted at Warriewood, North Narrabeen, Elanora Heights and then towards Cromer and Cromer Heights, as embers set alight bush near the War Veterans' home at Collaroy Plateau. Residents desperately fought to save their homes, packed belongings, especially the photo albums, as Sydney was engulfed in a pall of smoke. Ash and fragments of charred leaves fell in distant Manly. The fire pushed on towards St Ives and fire fighters rushed to Spencer on the Hawkesbury, West Pymble, Killara, Mona Vale, Tumbledown Dick, Ingleside and Terrey Hills, while the isolated residents on the Western Foreshores managed 'on their own', where day looked like night.

Backburning saved both Currawong and Great Mackerel beaches. Incredibly 'the whole peninsula from Newport to Palm Beach, and Scotland Island was potentially threatened'.

Many listened to the radio or watched the coverage on television. The closed highway north was lined with cars. Ferries and craft evacuated residents around Broken Bay and Pittwater. Many older residents were evacuated from retirement villages because of fire or smoke and all the 1600 residents of the War Veterans' home at Collaroy Plateau were evacuated when fire directly threatened the village. Evacuation centres were established at Mona Vale Surf Club and Mona Vale Memorial Hall, with other areas on stand by.

The aftermath of bush fires is the heart break of lost homes, some burned, while others miraculously survive, the loss of personal irreplaceable family treasures and the daunting prospect of rebuilding lives. In Warringah/Pittwater 231 hectares of land burned. Twenty seven houses and two units were totally destroyed and 60 houses and four units partially damaged. In addition cars, caravans, boats, garages and a range of property were lost bringing the total cost of the entire damage of property to $12,115,053. Without the enormous effort by fire fighters, with associated assistance from the NSW Fire Brigades, ACT Urban & Rural Fire brigades, National Parks & Wildlife Services, the Army, the RAN, the rural branch of the Country Fire Service, the Melbourne Metropolitan Fire Brigade and the Central Eastern Region Response Group, the cost may have been much higher.

Xanthorrheas *regenerate after the January 1994 bushfires, 27 January 1994. (Joe Murphy,* Manly Daily)

Snapperman Beach and Palm Beach wharf, with bushfire smoke in the background on the 8 January 1994. (Manly Daily)

PITTWATER COUNCIL

TODAY'S Pittwater local government area was part of Warringah Shire Council, established in 1906. Manly, incorporated in 1877, was a separate municipal area which derisively considered Warringah 'rabbit country'. Following World War II, improved traffic conditions and growing car ownership led to an increase in Warringah's population and the area became suburbanised. At that period it was believed larger local government areas led to better government, so much so that it seemed possible the whole northern region from Manly to Palm Beach could be one local government area. From the natural boundary of Narrabeen Lakes, the area north had its own character. In 1955 there was unrest when a group from North Balgowlah called for amalgamation with Manly Municipality. Manly was willing to absorb the southern area, C Riding, of Warringah. At the time Manly wished to claim city status.

By the 1960s Warringah was rapidly growing and in 1961 Councillor Fisher of Warringah saw advantages if the whole peninsula came under one council. Some considered Warringah too large an area and its headquarters at Brookvale were too far from Pittwater. *Pittwater Rising – The Making of Pittwater Council* by Pauline Curby is an overview and covers the path to secession.

During the 1960s separation of Warringah's A Riding (today's Pittwater Council) was supported by Des Creagh, an Avalon resident and Warringah Shire Councillor, together with a group of residents. Creagh formed the Pittwater Municipal Committee but submissions to various Ministers for Local Government fell on deaf ears. By 1985 the campaign attracted wider public support, due to controversies over various developments, particularly the construction of a multistorey building Delmege, at the corner of Mona Vale Road and Bungan Street. There was public antagonism to its height and size and public protest meetings held, one attracting a thousand people. The result was the emergence of the Peninsula Residents Council (PRC) as a powerful community organisation. An inquiry resulted in the dismissal of Warringah Shire Council, with an administrator appointed in December 1985.

When the Council was reinstated two years later Eric Green and Robert Dunn, both members of the PRC, were elected for the area north of Narrabeen Lagoon, with a mandate 'Urban Conservation and Local Government Reform'. Des Creagh and the PRC joined forces.

A petition of 12 000 signatures for a Boundaries Commission Inquiry for a new council was initially rejected. Later a petition of 20 000 signatures saw David Hay, Minister for Local Government, agree to the inquiry held in July 1990. Finally and unusually, a referendum of voluntary postal votes was held. Contrary to statistics, where in such circumstances only 20 per cent of voters respond, an amazing 73 per cent voted in favour of a new council.

On 1 May 1992 Pittwater Municipal Council was proclaimed by the NSW Government, the first Council for 100 years to be established as a result of petition and vote of the people. The first council election was on 24 October 1992 when Councillor Robert Dunn became Mayor of Pittwater.

Pittwater covers 125 square kilometres and its boundaries are Narrabeen Bridge to the south, the Tasman Sea to the east, Barrenjoey Headland to the north and Coal and Candle Creek to the west. The population is approximately 53 000. Pittwater Council's vision statement declares 'To be leaders in the provision of Local Government Services, to strive to conserve, protect and enhance the natural and built environment of Pittwater and to improve the quality of life for our community and for future generations'.

Palm Beach in 1950 with a relatively undeveloped hillside. In 1988 Bob Ellis wrote 'Like the Christmas holidays, Palm Beach is what Australians have instead of psycho-analysis.' (Warringah Library Local Studies)

CHRONOLOGY

Prior 1788 Territory of local Aborigines.

1788 Governor Phillip led first exploratory party to Broken Bay and named Pittwater for William Pitt, the Younger, Prime Minister of England.

1788–1790 Various explorations by Phillip and/or officers of First Fleet, including exploration and naming of the Hawkesbury River.

1789 Captain John Hunter surveyed Broken Bay and 'Pitt Water'.

1810 Scotland Island granted to emancipist, Andrew Thompson. Robert MacIntosh, Snr, farming at Pittwater.

1816 Naval surgeon, James Napper, granted 400 acres at Barrenjoey. Governor Macquarie inspected Pittwater farms.

1819 Robert Campbell granted 700 acres at Mona Vale.

1821 Henry Gasken received 50 acres with frontage on Careel Bay, confirmed in 1833. Peter Patullo held 80 acres at Bay View. David Foley settled on land, later site of Rock Lily.

1822 Bilgola Farm advertised.

1824 Mona Vale land grants.

1827 John Farrell granted 60 acres at Avalon.

1829 McCarrs Creek surveyed by William Govett.

1830s Land grants at Bayview, Crystal Bay, Careel Bay, Newport, Salt Pan Point, Taylors Point, Stokes Point, Mona Vale, Currawong, Great Mackerel Beach.

1832 James Jenkins permitted to occupy 700 acres at North Narrabeen. Father J J Therry granted 1200 acres, covering Whale Beach, Careel Bay, Salt Pan, Clareville, Avalon and Bilgola.

1834 William Lawson granted 640 acres at Lambert Peninsula (West Head).

1837 Father J J Therry 200 acres from Whale Beach to Newport.

1843 Customs House established at foot of Barrenjoey headland. John Farrell granted 60 acres at Long Beach, Newport.

1855 Joseph Bens/Binns and Charles Jenkins farming at Scotland Island.

1860 Father Therry unsuccessfully explored for coal at Avalon.

1862 Stone Customs House built at Barrenjoey, plus boatman's cottage, boathouse and stone jetty. Stewart Towers erected at Barrenjoey. Request for railway to Newport. Late 1860s Sally Morris arrived at Coasters Retreat.

1870s William Bede Dalley built house at Bilgola Beach.

1872 Methodist chapel built at Church Point. Coach service Manly to Newport established by C E Jeanerett and steamer excursions from Newport. Mona Vale to Church Point road surveyed, also Barrenjoey Road and Bayview Road.

1879 Wharf built at Newport.

1880 Jeannerett built Newport Hotel. William Boulton, first licensee of Newport Hotel. Narrabeen Bridge opened, replacing ford.

1881 Barrenjoey Lighthouse completed, with George Mulhall as lighthouse keeper. Collins' Retreat operating at Newport, later known as Bayview House amongst other names.

1882 Post Office opened at Bayview.

1886 Rock Lily Hotel rebuilt in brick by Leon Houreux.

1887 Church Point Wharf built. Jim Booth opened store and boats hired. Church Point chapel operated as school 1884–1888.

1888 Pittwater Public School and residence opened. St John the Baptist Church moved to Bayview Road.

1889 Newport School opened. Newport Telegraph office opened.

1890s Coaches operated between Manly and Pittwater in 1880s/1890s.

1891 'Lucinda' weekend by Committee drafting Commonwealth Constitution.

1892 Battle by 'pushes' at Newport Hotel. Inspection of area for Ku-ring-gai Chase.

1894 Ku-ring-gai Chase dedicated as national reserve. Barrenjoey School closed.

1896 First public telephone in Pittwater opened at Bayview. Bayview House became Scott's Boarding House.

1900 Barrenjoey Customs House closed. New stone school at Newport opened.

1901 Bayview Wharf built.

1904 Barrenjoey Post Office closed.

1905 Considerable settlement at Mona Vale and area had two stores.

1906 First motor omnibus service Manly to Newport. Warringah Shire boundaries proclaimed and first meeting of nominee Warringah Shire Council. Pittwater School at Bayview closed, pupils to Mona Vale. Scotland Island surveyed for auction. First Pittwater Regatta held.

1907 M. & Madame Briquet take over Rock Lily. Stone St John the Baptist Church opened at Mona Vale. Brock estate auctioned.

1911 Pittwater Public School opened.

1912 Land auctions at Palm Beach. Florida, Sunrise and Palm Beach Roads named.

1913 Cabbage Tree Club, Palm Beach built as private home for W Chorley. Tram line, via Pittwater Road, extended to Narrabeen. From 1913 to 1918 various land auctions – Newport, Careel Ocean Estate, Clareville, Bayview, Careel Bay and Bushrangers Hill.

1914–1918 First World War. Various homes built at Palm Beach, including many at 'Pill Hill,' during 1915–1916.

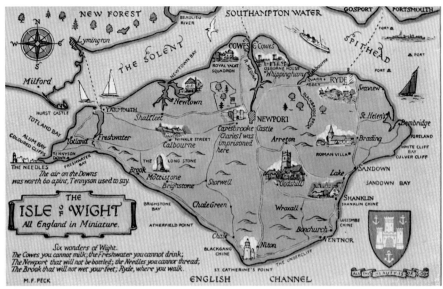

The Isle of Wight was a popular holiday place of Queen Victoria (Osborne House), and the origin of the names of some Sydney suburbs including Newport, Freshwater and Ryde. (Jim Boyce)

1919 Adolph Albers purchased land at Bungan Head. Built Bungan Castle from local stone.

1920 Barrenjoey Road bituminised and main road Palm Beach to Newport completed.

1920s The Orrs commence golf course at Bayview.

1921 First land subdivisions at Avalon. Palm Beach Surf Life Saving Club founded. Auctions at Whale Beach, Soldiers, Taylors and Church Points. Death on 6 June of Sally Morris, after 50 years at The Basin.

1922–1923 Land sales at Careel Bay, Great Mackerel Beach and Bilgola, Taylors Point and Newport.

1924 Palm Beach Golf Club formed.

1928 Plan mooted for separate Pittwater shire.

1920s Telegraph poles cut at Church Point. Development at Scotland Island, two roads, tennis court, three wharves, swimming baths.

1932 Church Point Chapel demolished amid protest. Sydney Harbour Bridge completed making access easier to Pittwater.

1936–1937 McCarrs Creek Road to Ku-ring-gai Chase constructed, together with various roads at Church Point.

1937–1938 The Wildlife Preservation Society bought land to preserve Angophora Reserve. Opened in 1938. Royal Prince Alfred Yacht Club established at Green Point. Wynyard to Palm beach bus service commenced operation.

1941 Defences built in Pittwater area, small vessels removed to distant areas. Various defence personnel in Pittwater. Brock's Folly used by military authorities.

1947 Oyster leases at Church Point. Boom period of glass houses with 3,500 at Warriewood/Mona Vale.

1948 Rock Lily Hotel restored.

1950 Avalon Beach Public School opened.

1951 Avalon Beach Public School officially opened.

1955 Regular ferry services within Pittwater.

1958 Bushfire at Elanora and Ingleside.

1961 The Baha'i Temple dedicated and opened.

1963 Pittwater High School opened.

1964 Mona Vale Hospital opened in March.

1966 Proposal made by 88 residents of A Riding to secede from Warringah Shire Council. Original Mona Vale school demolished.

1968 Barrenjoey High School opened.

1971 Warringah Council to allow no further subdivision on western shores of Pittwater.

1975 Site of Zoo farm rezoned as residential, light development and recreation area.

1976 Barrenjoey Customs House destroyed by fire.

1985 Protests concerning multi-storey Delmege development at Mona Vale. Warringah Shire Council dismissed and an Administrator appointed.

1990 Petition signed by 20 000 for an inquiry for separate Council. Local Government Boundaries Commission conducted a non-compulsory pool of electors, with 73% voting in favour of secession.

1992 Pittwater Council proclaimed on 1 May 1992.

2004 Concern over proposed changes to Mona Vale Hospital. Development of Warriewood area.

2006 NSW Government announced a new hospital would be built at Frenchs Forest, stating Mona Vale Hospital will remain open. Final section of Warriewood Wetlands boardwalk officially opened.

BIBLIOGRAPHY

Attenbrow, V, *Sydney's Aboriginal Past*, UNSW Press, 2002

Baha'i Temple brochure and website

Barry, Hugh, *A History of the Elanora Country Club*, Elanora Country Club, 1977

Bosler, Nan, *Terry Hills General Store*, Local History Resource Unit, Narrabeen Community Learning Centre, 1992.

Bosler, Nan, *The Fascinating History of Pittwater*, Local History Resource Unit, Pittwater Council, March, 1997

Brawley, Sean, *Beach Beyond – A History of the Palm Beach Surf Club 1921–1996*, UNSW Press, 1996

Burton, Craig, *Barrenjoey Peninsula & Pittwater Heritage Study*, Vol.1, Study Report, January 1989, McDonald, McPhee Pty Ltd

Champion, Shelagh & George, *Did the Aborigines of the Manly, Warringah and Pittwater Peninsula Really Belong to the Ku-ring-gai Tribe?*

Champion, Shelagh & George, *Manly Warringah & Pittwater 1850–1880*, 1998

Curby, Pauline, *Pittwater Rising – The Making of Pittwater Council*, Pittwater Council, 2002

Dixon, Jean, *The Riddle of Powderworks Road*, Wentworth Books Pty Ltd, 1980

Fairley, Alan, *The Beaten Track, A Guide to the Bushland Around Sydney*, 1972

Fairley, Alan, *Along the Track, A Guide to the Bushland Around Sydney*, 1974

Gillen, Mollie, *The Founders of Australia, A Biographical Dictionary of the First Fleet*, Library of Australian History, 1989

Gould, Sue, *Coasters Retreat Pittwater, Recollections and Historical Notes*, Kingsclear Books, 1993

Hunt, Mrs Muriel (nee Small) Private letter to Joan Lawrence, 1985

Macken, Jim, *The Wreck of the Hazard & other true sea stories of Broken Bay*, James Macken, 1994

Macken, Jim, *Sally Morris of The Basin*, James Macken, 2001

Macken, Jim, *Martin Burke, The Father of Pittwater*, 2nd edition, James Macken, 2005

Macken Jim, *Pittwater's War*, James Macken, 2005

Macleod, Virginia, *Burnt Out? Experiences of the January 1994 Bush Fires in Warringah and Pittwater*, Local History Resource Unit, 1996

Manly Warringah Journal of Local History, Vol. 1, No.3, April 1988; Volume 1, No. 3, April 1988; Vol. 1, No. 4, September 1988; Vol. 5, No. 1, 'Mona Vale, An historical account of people and places', November 1992; Vol. 6, March 1995

Narrabeen Local History Resource Unit, *Manly Warringah People Places & Pastimes*, 1986

Norman, Graeme, *Yachting & The Royal Prince Alfred Yacht Club*, Child & Associates, 1988

Park, Ruth, *The Companion Guide to Sydney*, Collins, 1973

Peninsula News, Warren Whitfield's official Aboriginal welcome at the Woy Woy Australia Day celebrations, February 2002

Pittwater Library Service, Local Studies Information

Revitt, Jim, The History of Pittwater Council, Pittwater Council website, www.pittwaterlga.com.au

Roberts, Jan, *Maybanke Anderson: Sex, suffrange & social reform*, Hale & Iremonger, 1993

Roberts, Jan, Ed., *Avalon, Landscape & Harmony, Walter Burley Griffin, Alexander Stewart Jolly & Harry Ruskin Rowe*, Ruskin Rowe Press, 1999

Smith, Keith Vincent, *King Bungaree – A Sydney Aborigine meets the great South Pacific Explorers, 1799–1830*, Kangaroo Press, 1992

Sparks, Jervis, *Tales from Barranjoey*, Jervis Sparks, 1992

Sparks, Jervis, *The Red Light of Palm Beach*, Jervis Sparks, 2006

Spearritt, Peter, *Sydney Since the Twenties*, Hale & Iremonger, 1978

Steege, Joan, Ed., *Palm Beach 1788–1988*, The Palm Beach Association, 1988

Sun, Sand and Surf, Memories of the Northern Beaches, Warringah Shire Council, 1995

Sydney Morning Herald, Good Weekend Magazine, 18 March, 2006

The Warringah Bicentennial Coastal Walk, brochures produced by the Parks and Recreation Branch of Warringah Shire Council, 1988

Tatz, Colin, *A Course of History, Monash Country Club, 1931–2001*, Allen & Unwin, 2002

Turbet, Peter *The Aborigines of the Sydney District before 1788*, Kangaroo Press, 1989

Warringah Heritage Study, Vol.1, Reports – Historical Context Reports, Landscape Report, Extracts from April 1994, Hughes Trueman Ludlow, 33 Atchison Street, St Leonards

INDEX

AVAILABLE AT ALL GOOD BOOKSTORES AND NEWSAGENTS. IF UNAVAILABLE PLEASE PHONE (02) 9557 4367

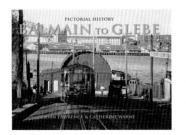

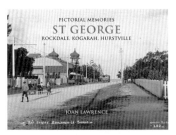

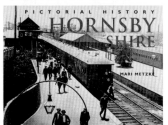
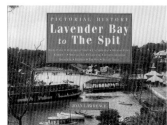

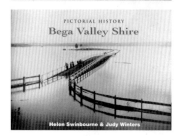
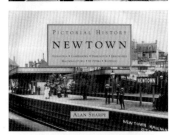

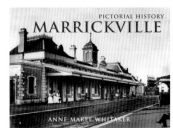

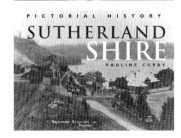

Also available South Sydney, Holroyd and Hawkesbury

Kingsclear Books PO Box 335, Alexandria NSW 1435. Email kingsclear@wr.com.au www.kingsclearbooks.com.au